KV-050-330

Toward Jazz

André Hodeir

Toward Jazz

Translated by Noel Burch

A DACAPO PAPERBACK

Library of Congress Cataloging in Publication Data

Hodeir, André, 1921–
    Toward jazz.

    (A Da Capo paperback)
    Reprint. Originally published: New York: Grove Press, 1962.
    Includes bibliographical references and index.
    1. Jazz music — Addresses, essays, lectures. I. Title.
ML3507.H6   1986   785.42   85-46071
ISBN 0-306-80264-3 (pbk.)

This Da Capo Press paperback edition of *Toward Jazz* is an unabridged
republication of the edition published in New York in 1962. It is
reprinted by arrangement with the author.

Published by Da Capo Press, Inc.
A Subsidiary of Plenum Publishing Corporation
233 Spring Street, New York, N.Y. 10013

Other books by André Hodeir

Jazz: Its Evolution and Essence
Since Debussy: A View of Contemporary Music

CONTENTS

PART FOUR / ON WORKS

PART FIVE / LISTENING NOTES

PART SIX / PROSPECTS OF JAZZ

FOREWORD

M y previous book, *Jazz: Its Evolution and Essence,* was
the fruit of reflections on the general problems of jazz; it
was an analytical book, and might have displayed a certain
serenity of attitude had its author not been involved, to some
extent, in the aesthetic quarrels of the period. *Toward Jazz*
is not entirely above the fray, either, but here the polemic
aspect has undergone a fundamental change. Henceforward,
I feel, our most urgent task is to reappraise the individual
jazz musician, examining both his strengths and weaknesses.
The greatest jazz artists have, at times, displayed attitudes
toward their audience which would have been despised by a
Beethoven, a Van Gogh, or a Kafka. So far no one has ever
set forth the motives for their behavior with any conviction.
My ambiguous situation—I am not a full-fledged member of
the jazz community but neither am I a complete outsider—
does not allow me to defend a form of ethics which I cannot
bring myself to adopt. All I can do is sound the alarm, raise
a cry of revolt. Thus, *Toward Jazz* reflects my personal concerns far more than any of my previous books. This may be
why more space is devoted to setting forth a line of thought
and less to actual argumentation. I am no longer concerned,
as I used to be, with objectivity; I am trying to define a truly
personal attitude toward the phenomenon of jazz.

In this sense, *Toward Jazz* may be regarded as a transitional book. The point of departure of this collection—as expressed in articles written some time ago—is the conception of jazz found in *Jazz: Its Evolution and Essence;* its last chapters, however, reveal other horizons which are to be further explored in *The Worlds of Jazz.* Thus, this book both describes a change and bridges a gap.

Various considerations have gradually led me to adopt new aims and methods. The chief external reason for this change is that jazz criticism is no longer, as it was when I began to write, a desert peopled with dinosaurs whom we naively credited with the agility of mountain goats. Constructive work has been done since, and certain things may now be considered as established. An exhausting reappraisal was most urgent then, and this required a Cartesian skepticism. The task at hand today, however, calls for the visionary outlook of a Nietzsche.

A number of personal reasons may have played a greater role in this modification. I spent the early months of 1957 in the jazz milieus of New York, working with the musicians and trying to share their fascinating, eccentric lives. Had I been able to adjust myself to that strange world, had I not rejected the communion of narcotics, had I been able to rid myself of my cultural background, everything would have been so simple: I could have become the authorized spokesman for one of the most remarkable groups of contemporary artists. But I could not and would not take that irreversible plunge. I floated about on the surface, contemplating those incomprehensible creatures who would occasionally emerge from the depths to wave or even beckon to me. I was able to communicate with John Lewis because, even when our opinions differed, our cultural backgrounds brought us together; Monk's thought processes, however, remained a closed book for me, and had our musical affinities not given me a sudden, intuitive grasp of his universe, I might well have passed him up altogether.

And yet my stay in New York has a symbolic meaning for me. I look upon it less as an experience in human relations or as a period of technical study, than as a crucial moment in my musical life. Two or three years earlier, I had emerged from a period of deliberate creative silence that went back to the early fifties. In New York, just as I began to feel excluded from the world of jazzmen, I also realized that I was able to play what I regard as an effective role in the creative development of jazz. My articles—those that appear in this volume—were no longer mere critical introductions (like the "listening notes" at the end of this collection); they were gradually moving toward a form of poetic meditation, almost invariably inspired by the musicians who have most influenced my work: Duke Ellington, Gil Evans, Milt Jackson, Thelonious Monk.

The reader may regret this development, but it was inevitable. I have never been one of those professional critics who can turn out a brilliant article on a fashionable subject at the drop of a hat. The most severely objective analyses in *Jazz: Its Evolution and Essence* already stemmed from an inward, personal necessity. During the period in which I abstained from any form of creation, my desire to elucidate the fundamental components of jazz was significant in itself. My efforts may have been of help to jazz lovers, but they were useful to at least one musician as well, and that was myself. Though it may not have been outwardly apparent, this underlying tendency was already implicit in my choice of subject matter. At the time, many readers were surprised at my having dealt with certain subjects and omitted others altogether. "This book is not an encyclopedia," I wrote, in order, I expect, to forestall discussion on this point. The burden of

objectivity was growing heavy to bear. Already a few exceptionally keen observers could tell from the very patterns of
the book that I might one day abandon general topics and
write about just one aspect of a musician or his work, an
aspect which would have a special significance for me. How
much more exhilarating is this new form of commitment
compared with sterile, sectarian polemics.

There is no point in writing about music unless one
"writes in blood" as Nietzsche demanded. Seen in this light,
the phrase "write about . . ." seems tainted somehow. By its
very nature, any truly poetic commentary should be so
thoroughly *appropriate* that it would be indecent to describe
it as an article *about* something.

The specialist's ambition should be to write, not a book
"about jazz," but a "jazz book." My readers will no doubt
see how far I still am from this goal, but in the best pages of
Toward Jazz they may also appreciate my efforts to approach it. (By the best pages I mean those which are the
least "objective," those in which I am most present, in which
I come closest to integrating my own ideas into the subject,
those, I might almost say, in which I speak my own language, leaving behind me, once and for all, quarrels which
are revived for the last time in the oldest and least integrated
pieces in this volume: chapters 4 and 5.)

The articles in this collection appeared between 1953 and
1959 in the following periodicals: *Jazz Hot* (Paris), *Arts*
(Paris), *The Jazz Review* (New York), *Down Beat* (Chi-
cago), *Jazz, A Quarterly of American Music* (Berkeley), as
well as in two anthologies: *This Is Jazz* (Ken Williamson,
ed.; London, Newnes, 1960) and *The Art of Jazz* (Martin T.
Williams, ed.; New York, Oxford University Press, 1959).
They have undergone no major changes; I have merely cor-
rected any typographical and factual errors found in reading

them over. Other, more serious errors—errors of judgment for the most part—are indicated in notes¹ which also give my present opinion. The reader, I hope, will take a humorous view of the contradictions arising from the juxtaposition of articles dating from different periods. These contradictions do—or did—exist; it would have been unworthy to conceal them. In conclusion, I wish to thank all those who have given me their helpful advice and suggestions: Jeanne Bisilliat-Gardet, Henri Bernard, Noel Burch, Leonard Murray, Lucien Malson, and Martin T. Williams.

¹ These "self-critical" notes, as well as other particulars, will be found in the Appendix, p. 211 ff. The reader's attention will be called to them by numbers in brackets [ ].

Part One

On Jazzmen

CHAPTER 1

The Bird Is Gone

A tribute to Charlie Parker

Charlie Parker was the youngest of the musicians known as the "Three Great Men of Jazz," and yet he has been the first to leave us. His death is an irreparable loss to the world of jazz.[1]

Charlie Parker was unquestionably jazz's greatest saxophonist and probably, with Louis Armstrong, its greatest improviser. His contributions were so significant, his discoveries so revolutionary, that more than ten years of modern jazz have not sufficed to exhaust their novelty; one may even say that Parker's art contains musical and emotional potentialities which have not yet been fully exploited by younger musicians.

Any truly revolutionary artist is invariably accused of intellectualism. People who are not touched by a new form of sensibility always blame it on the new form and never on their own unreceptiveness. In his first records, the Bird was often accused of lacking warmth and even of being a show-off! Time has proven how unfounded these reproaches were.

As one became increasingly familiar with Parker's work, its emotional drive became more and more apparent, dispelling any reservation one might have had. Today it would never occur to anyone to speak of *Parker's Mood* or *Embraceable You* as "intellectual" music.

On a purely musical level, Charlie Parker freed jazz of a number of trammels. He had the courage to challenge aesthetic axioms which were tending to become frozen dogma. It was he who first brought to jazz that disturbing discontinuity of rhythm and melody upon which some of his finest works were based. And though perfectly able to play jazz that was calm and rhythmically "in place," he threw himself with mad audacity into a conception of phrasing which did away almost entirely with the regular beat and which he was able to provide with the indispensable points of support only through his remarkable sense of rhythmic continuity. No one has ever gone so far as Parker in the expression of aural tension, and no one else has been able to produce a tone so splendid that it defied all the traditional notions of beauty and ugliness.

This is the side of Parker's music which will probably remain the most precious and most inaccessible. We shall never forget that it was he who showed us the gateway to a world bordering on musical madness—and I mean madness, not lunacy—and will always regret that he couldn't persuade us to follow him through it. For we must not deceive ourselves: his influence has not been as far-reaching as was generally supposed a few years ago. If Parker had any followers at all, they took their cue from his most accessible music, the gay, relaxed pieces such as *Scrapple from the Apple*. Bud Powell and Clifford Brown were perhaps the only musicians to have grasped the essence of

Parker's message, capturing in their faster pieces the echo of that torrent of sound that was his *Ko-Ko*.

I did not know Charlie Parker personally, but I feel that I did understand him fairly well. He is the only jazz musician who convinced me of the deep inner necessity of his art on the very first hearing. Armstrong and Ellington had been the authentic jazz spokesmen of their generation; it was the Bird who provided ours with its highest aesthetic justification. He carried on the jazz tradition and transformed it at one and the same time. He once told a reporter: "Bop [read: "my music"] is no love-child of jazz"; this was more than just a quip, it was a proud assertion that he had succeeded in creating a world apart. Parker was aware of his own genius, knew that he had carried jazz onto a highly personal plane, just as Dostoevsky, Joyce, and Kafka carried the novel into spheres beyond the reach of the average man. Not that we can take this statement literally—throughout his career Parker gave ample proof that he was a "child of jazz"—but neither can we fail to see its deeper meaning. It was probably because his music was so inaccessible—by comparison with the immediate "popular" appeal of an Armstrong or a Bechet—that the Bird was condemned to a life of hardship. In order to earn a living, this gifted, authentic artist was obliged to play incredible hack tunes that purblind and tone-deaf managers made him record in the fallacious hope of cashing in on a reputation earned among his fellow jazzmen and brought to public attention by the press.

Yes, I know, Parker might have refused. Perhaps the man lacked the stature of the artist. That happens. But to me, who never knew him, it seems self-evident that Parker, whether he was courageous or cowardly, intelligent or stupid, suffered more than we can know perhaps, from the isolation in which his genius had placed him. He was destined to owe the best part of his reputation to the worst part of a body of music, which, at its finest, opened up a whole new world of ideas and emotions. This may have been the cause of the disorders in his life and also, perhaps, the explanation of his death.

CHAPTER 2

Why Do They Age So Badly?

When a fan once asked Louis Armstrong's manager whether Louis wasn't going to retire soon, he is said to have expressed genuine surprise and have answered: "What do you mean, retire? Why Louis's making three thousand dollars a week now!"[2]

Though the story may be apocryphal, it does convey a deep truth about the history of jazz, past and present.

For the history of both jazz and jazzmen is that of creative purity gradually corrupted by success. In his youth, the great jazz musician has to struggle to impose his art; if he succeeds in doing so, he must then struggle daily *against* his own success. How many men have won *this* struggle? Charlie Parker undoubtedly did, because he never reached the peak of success and because he died at the age of thirty-five. Monk and Miles Davis may win it, either because of their tough, incorruptible characters, or because they took Pascal's advice and fled success rather than try to stand up to it.

What did life hold in store for those who really made good, for the aristocrats of jazz, the celebrities? An unremitting decline, an inevitable subsidence into complacency. None has been able to hold himself aloof from fame, none has the will power to break out of the magic circle of money, none has been able to find himself again. The same process occurs over and over again (and we've not seen the end of the farce; modern jazz musicians won't fare any better than their elders): first, the young musician expresses himself freely, breaks the rules, disconcerting and even shocking his listeners; then the public adopts him, he attracts disciples and becomes a star. He thinks he is still free, but he has become a prisoner. He no longer has time to exist as an individual; he has to travel, he has to play—tonight in one town, tomorrow in another—he has to honor his contracts. As his creative powers decline, he clings to his past achievements, not daring to budge. When this happens what is there left for him to do but, as Roger Guérin wrote, "drag about from one town to the next the remains of what was once genius or great talent."[1]

How can the jazzman escape this fate? The greater he is, the harder it seems to hit him. A man who has been so completely dominated by life as to have become a goose with golden eggs can hardly hope to maintain that separation between art and life which is at the origin of all great creation. This will be true even if he manages to avoid any commercial concessions (and that is a difficult achievement). For how can he find the time to *renew himself?* And if he cannot renew himself, how can he avoid the boredom of repetition?

There is not a single great soloist who hasn't experienced this form of boredom, which is particularly rampant among jazzmen. There is no doubt but what it can destroy the creative influx of the most gifted artists. And when he no

---

[1] From an interview with this French trumpet player, *Jazz Hot,* No. 128, January, 1958.

longer has anything new to say, he is likely to stop "getting a kick" out of playing; this is the worst thing that can happen to a jazzman. He may be able to revive his enjoyment temporarily, but its return can be even more painful than its absence, for, in the meantime, the artist's creative powers may well have vanished for good. This may have been the case with Django Reinhardt, the greatest of all European improvisers, who, only a few weeks before his death, muttered: "The guitar bores me." And yet Django had been able to take a detached view of his life, give up a successful career which had begun to weary him, and retreat into a private universe which at least had the merit of purity (his painting, independent of its strengths and weaknesses, attests to this).

Like every tragedy, this one has a comic side. It is well-known that the general public is seldom quick to grasp the discoveries of an artist. Thus, only when a musician has fallen as low as he can, when he has *absolutely nothing left to say,* when he is drained and exhausted, then and only then does he reach the pinnacle of success, only then is he hailed as an undisputed genius.

Since, in addition, every European country—and France in particular—is ten years behind the times as far as jazz is concerned, it is perfectly natural that for the average Frenchman the great names of jazz are men in their fifties or sixties, whose firmly established fame may be a highly fitting reward for their past achievement—this is true at least of Armstrong and Ellington—but is justified by nothing they have done in the past ten years.

Jazz has one thing in common with sports: it requires its performers—especially drummers and trumpet players—to be in first-rate physical condition. But in sports it is the actual result that counts first and foremost, and the aging athlete is *obliged* to retire. In jazz, on the other hand, competition exists only on the level of the jam session, that modern form of the old cutting contest; here, sentiment plays a preponderant role with the judges (or listeners) who, in practice, seldom repudiate their traditional idols. If relations between a sporting champion and his fans were governed by the same law, Jack Dempsey and Bill Tilden would still be the most popular heroes of the sporting world, and the general public would be only barely aware of the existence of Joe Louis and Jaroslaw Drobny.

Though to some this comparison may seem disrespectful, it will perhaps serve to pry open reluctant eyes. Of course, one may counter that Tilden was undoubtedly a greater tennis player than Drobny, or that Louis may never have equalled Dempsey for sheer class. I don't deny this. I do not claim that the young jazzmen are intrinsically better than their elders. I simply wish to make clear that the vital elements in jazz are today's musicians and not yesterday's. What is more, it can be shown that most of the great names in jazz, the big box office draws, are musicians who, though truly creative at one time perhaps, can no longer be regarded as anything but entertainers. Worse still, they are *imitators*, and bad imitators at that because, as a final touch of irony, they are reduced to imitating themselves.

Thus we find a situation in jazz comparable to that of contemporary music. Except for the mink coats and limousines, what is the difference between the crowds that cheer the mummified "kings" of jazz and those that trustingly applaud the meaningless string of works that Igor Stravinsky is now turning out with a pen that, many years ago, was so gifted? Jazz is full of Stravinskys of every shape and size.

Trusting applause can be sincere as well. In 1950 Paris

fans applauded "on trust" the great trumpeter Roy Eldridge at a time when he was already well on the decline. Ten
or fifteen years earlier, at the height of his creative period,
he would have been completely ignored—just as another
Roy Eldridge was ignored three years later in the same hall,
when Clifford Brown's gifts, then in full bloom, went entirely unnoticed. That night everyone was enthralled by a
"monstre sacré" named Lionel Hampton, another ghost
whose frantic acrobatics succeeded in hiding from most people the hopeless sterility of his music.

Must we conclude that, for the general public, true creation is the most unbearable of all phenomena—when it is not
simply *invisible*—whereas with the passing of time a pale
reflection of it will, in all sincerity, be considered the most
pleasurable?

Can it be that twenty years from now, when Lionel Hampton is completely forgotten, delirious audiences will be cheer-
ing a gray-bearded Milt Jackson? For if the youth of the
future resembles that of today, they will respect only the
music of their grandfathers and no longer be disturbed by
Milt Jackson because he will have ceased to be creative.

Let us hope that this will not happen; let us hope that
Milt Jackson (or Miles Davis or Thelonious Monk) does
not wind up clowning in Broadway theaters or Paris music
halls, but just goes on being the great musician that he is;
let us hope that he does not become a matinee idol but con-
tinues to create. And since we are in a utopian mood, let us
also hope that the widest possible audience will go to hear
him play, as well as Miles and Monk and all the other great
jazzmen of their times, hear them play *in their time* which
may not last very much longer—which may in fact already
be finished.

CHAPTER 3

Why Did Ellington "Remake" His Masterpiece?

Duke Ellington holds a privileged position in the history of jazz.[3] He was its first *composer* in the strict sense of the term, and for a long time he was its only composer. Fats Waller was not a composer, he merely *wrote tunes*. Ernie Wilkins is an *arranger* who works with other people's ideas. A composer is a musician who makes full use of a capacity which neither the tune writer nor, with very few exceptions, the arranger possesses, a capacity which might be defined as that of *endowing jazz with an additional dimension*. This dimension, which gives a work new depth and greater possibilities for development, is form. Jazz history may be summed up as follows: Armstrong created jazz, Ellington created form in jazz; Parker and Davis re-created jazz, while Monk is trying to re-create form in jazz.

In order to create his music, the Duke forged himself a double-edged tool. On the one hand, he had a flair for orchestration and handled tone color imaginatively; by working on these natural gifts he was able to transform them into an orchestral language. On the other, he benefited by that respect which a band leader can earn by combining a smiling authority with an indisputable musical superiority; he used it to build an orchestra which, for fifteen years, was absolutely unique in jazz. His musical language was as integral a part of his orchestra as his orchestra was of the works he produced. There may have been other jazzmen with the equipment necessary to equal the Duke as a composer, but if so they lacked the organizational flair necessary to create a means of expressing themselves. Anyone can bring a score to a bandleader; the only way to be really creative in jazz is to have an orchestra at one's disposal. And if one has built that orchestra all by oneself, one may be in a position to make a substantial contribution to the language of jazz. Having an orchestra at one's disposal is not sufficient, however. Don Redman, Fletcher Henderson, Sy Oliver, and several others have attempted to break new ground in the field of form, which had been by-passed by the early jazzmen. Their praiseworthy efforts, however, lacked any deeply felt inspiration. It was thanks to Duke Ellington that we have been able to avoid doing the same spade work over again today. Single-handed he changed the face of a desert and brought forth the first fruit of that multidimensional music which may one day supplant every other form of jazz; and though at times the fruits were bitter, at others they were sweet indeed.

Duke Ellington was a brilliant precursor, though he hit his full stride in only a few, rare instances, as against hundreds of errors (errors which were nevertheless full of original touches and partial achievements); the Duke was once a great musician, but now fatigue seems to have gotten the best of him.

I understand the reasons for this fatigue, but I must also observe its effects. What I cannot bear is to watch Ellington the middle-aged bandleader debase the work of Ellington the artist. The fact that for the past ten years he has written nothing worth-while—has so declined, in fact, that there have been doubts that he actually wrote certain pieces of trash signed Ellington—would not in itself be very exceptional. Composers as great as Stravinsky, Bartók, and Schönberg each reached the point in their careers where they mysteriously seemed to lose their best creative powers forever. With Ellington, however, one would have thought that even after the creator in him had succumbed to the exhausting life he has led, the musician would survive. The Duke had been the only composer; we would still have liked to regard him as the greatest orchestra leader.

And yet two years ago. . . but this is a sorrowful tale. The directors of a large recording firm persuaded Ellington to record a set of pieces taken from his past. The idea was a rather poor one to begin with, but did have a positive side which might have deserved serious thought. After all, works as rich in sound texture as *In a Mellotone* or *Ko-Ko* might well reveal new dimensions when enhanced with the glamour of high fidelity.

I wish to call the reader's attention to the last-named piece. As he must know, the original version of *Ko-Ko* was recorded in 1940; it constitutes the most perfect example of Duke Ellington's language (then at the height of its development) and remains one of the undisputed masterpieces of orchestral jazz. Every jazz fan knows the 1940 *Ko-Ko* by heart.

This is where our story takes a preposterous turn, for as it happens there was at least one man who had forgotten that unique moment of beauty in the history of jazz, and that man was Duke Ellington himself! So far as I know, neither Rembrandt nor Cézanne ever did a watered-down copy of an early painting containing a vision that was already perfect in itself. Great works of architecture have, it is true, been altered, but the architects were already dead when this was done. The Duke has done *Ko-Ko* over again, and the result is a hideous copy which makes a mockery of his own masterpiece. Moreover, he has allowed this new version to be issued on a record, the mere title of which—*Historically Speaking*— is an insult to his great name.[1]

The whole thing is so unthinkable that I am assailed by a doubt: perhaps he did it purposely, in a conscious effort at self-debunking. In that case this article would be ludicrous, and there would be nothing left for me but to crawl into a hole for having written it. But then, who has ever attained such a summit of greatness? Not even Nietzsche. No, I'm afraid that the obvious explanation of this desecration is not a credit to Ellington. There is only one possible alternative: either the Duke has simply lost the remarkable musical sensibility which lay at the heart of his genius, or else he was never really conscious of the beauty of his music.

My love and respect for Duke Ellington and his music make me inclined to doubt this last hypothesis. The contemporary artist has one anguishing advantage over his predecessors, and this is a sense of historical perspective which enables him to situate himself with regard to the past. Duke Ellington is not a pure creature of instinct like Armstrong or Parker; whether we like it or not, every composer is an intellectual, a person capable of meditation. I should hate to think that Ellington never knew *who he was*. And if he did know, how can he have forgotten? Can he have lost, not only his creative powers, but his musical awareness as well, becoming oblivious to his own mistakes—I should say, his *crimes?*

But the hardest part of my task remains undone. I hope

---

[1] Bethlehem BCP 60.

no one will think I am performing it with the bitter gusto that one can take in pulling down minor idols; Jimmy Noone and Mezz Mezzrow are mere straw men; we are dealing here with something that was once very important.[4] I was a very young musician when I first heard Ellington's *Ko-Ko* sixteen years ago, and I immediately succumbed to the magic spell of that long-awaited vision. Suddenly I saw jazz in a new light; Ellington's music had reached fulfillment at last, and there was reason to hope that this achievement foreshadowed the revelation of an even more exciting musical universe.

The years have passed and the Duke's music has failed to keep its promise, but it would be unfair to hold this against him; the important thing, after all, is the tremendous contribution he did make. (I cannot help smiling when I think of the indignant article I published after the Duke's stay in Paris in 1950; my anger at his decline was justified, but in giving vent to it, I lacked proper perspective. This is not the case today, however, for the matter at hand is far more serious.)

The 1940 version of *Ko-Ko* was splendidly strange and violent.[2] The introduction seemed to come from another world, while Tricky Sam's (Joe Nanton) solo had a wail that was more than merely exotic, and even the Duke's piano had an unearthly sound to it. Above all, this was the first time that anyone had really *written for a jazz orchestra*; the beauty of Blanton's famous break was due entirely to the rigorous conception that had guided the Duke's hand throughout the previous choruses.

Listening to the 1956 version of *Ko-Ko* is one of the most painful ordeals imaginable to anyone for whom jazz and

---

[2] RCA Victor LPM 1715.

music are *living* experiences. Nothing is left of the qualities I have just mentioned (very briefly, I'm afraid, but then every jazz fan, I hope, will know what I'm talking about), nothing save an atrocious caricature. What was once magnificent becomes grotesque, the epic spirit gives way to stupid gesticulation, and the sense of mystery to mere vulgarity. Yet scarcely a note of the score itself has been changed. Never have two *versions* of a single piece constituted two such different *works*; only in jazz, I feel, is such a distortion of creative concept possible. What is unbelievable is that both versions should be the work of one and the same musician. One may object that Ellington no longer had the same musicians at his disposal. Tricky Sam and Blanton are dead. But in that case he shouldn't have re-recorded *Ko-Ko*! Whichever way you look at it, the Duke alone is responsible. In 1956 he had good material at his disposal. Quentin Jackson is a very respectable trombonist. The burden of his disgraceful, buffoonish interpretation of a solo which constituted one of the high points of Tricky Sam's career, must be borne by the Duke as well, for it was he who put Jackson in an impossible situation from the very moment when he snapped his fingers for the down-beat.

This is the crucial point. The reader does not realize, perhaps, that this moment of a performance, which does not appear on a recording, determines in one out of two cases the quality of the work about to be played. If the leader does not hit the right *tempo*, if his finger-snapping is a bit too slow or a bit too fast, his musicians will be thrown off balance with little hope of recovery. A bandleader worthy of the name almost always sets the right tempo at the very outset. In 1940 the Duke had a marvelous intuitive grasp of his composition; the tempo chosen was just right and his orchestra, which didn't always "swing it" (*In a Mellotone* was one of many pieces spoiled by a drummer who sounded like a frustrated drum major), immediately hit the right pace. The 1940 version of *Ko-Ko* remains one of the most swinging records of the swing era. As for the *Ko-Ko* of 1956...

What can possibly have happened? I don't think this disaster can be explained by practical considerations. Had recording techniques shrunk as they developed, making it necessary to play the arrangement in a shorter space of time, the Duke's decision to speed up his tempo would have been understandable, though not acceptable. If the Duke had not had the old recording at his disposal, one might think he had simply made an equally inexcusable error of judgment. Why this insane choice? Perhaps the Duke wanted to prove that his present orchestra had greater technical virtuosity than the earlier group; I find this unbelievable, but if it is true, what a dismal failure for the sake of such a trivial demonstration!

None of these explanations is satisfactory. No, there is only one possible reason for this choice, and that is a *diminution of musical sensibility*; it would not be the first time I have encountered such a thing.[3] How can a great musician have become so insensitive? I cannot carry this explanation any further, for the truth is that the whole thing is as puzzling to me as it is painful. I can only observe the results of the Duke's choice and these are disastrous.

---

[3] Does anyone remember what happened to Trummy Young's famous trombone solo on *Margie* (which he once recorded with Jimmy Lunceford), when he played it last year [1957] at the Olympia with Louis Armstrong? Here again the notes were exactly the same, but the tempo was such that what had once been a supple play of ambiguities now became a mere skeleton, devoid of any musical meaning. True, it was only Trummy Young.

Not only is Quentin Jackson's solo made *impossible* (as against Tricky Sam's, which we cannot avoid hearing "in our head"), but the whole arrangement is *inevitably* performed in a jarring, jerky style devoid of any swing. Ellington's broad phrasing can no longer draw its deep, even breath, but gasps and pants laboriously; once lovely figures are now twisted and contorted, a veil of ugliness has fallen over the work as a whole.

What did the Duke have to say about all this? Did he stand helplessly by, watching this farcical desecration of what ought to be his favorite score? Did he rush into the studio to put a stop to it, begin again from scratch, or even. . . call the whole thing off? Not a bit of it. He had already accepted—or even suggested—two "improvements" on the original, two changes which could not fail to disfigure it: a ridiculous introduction on the drums, and an affected clarinet solo which now dominates that stupendous fourth orchestral chorus (which, in the earlier version, was punctuated by percussive piano work of a splendidly aggressive character). After that, what was to stop him from ruining his own music completely with a bad choice of tempo? And why should he object to the record being issued?

For me, the title *Historically Speaking* means "The Duke Judged by His Past."[5] I'll never forget the musician who did the original *Ko-Ko*, but now I can never forget the one who agreed to sign this new version. I hope I've made myself clear. This is not just another bad record, it is the sign of a dereliction which confirms once and for all the decadence of a great musician.

We have the right to demand a great deal only of those who have done great things. There should be no doubt about it; the present article constitutes an unprecedented tribute to the Duke in his golden age. But it is also meant to put the reader on his guard against the enticements of a once glorious name which now represents only an endless succession of mistakes. This was the most ghastly mistake of all, for nothing can ever redeem it.

Part Two

On Criticism

CHAPTER 4

Letter on Evolutionism
and the Role of Criticism

> . . . an audience that will take the
> trouble to listen and learn before
> it criticizes.
> —*Igor Stravinsky*

> Preceded as we were by a genera-
> tion of illiterates, are we to become
> a crop of technocrats?
> —*Pierre Boulez*

1

DEAR SIR,

Boris Vian recently gave you rather rough handling, and you no doubt deserved some of what you got.[6] I do not wish to embroider on his vengeful tirade, but to examine, through your letter, the causes of the confusion which, as he says, prevails in the minds of many. I do not feel it is a waste of time to go into this problem in greater detail, since I myself must assume part of the responsibility for this confusion; after all, who can be responsible for it, if not those who write about jazz? Moreover, except for the reasonable tone in which it is couched, your letter might have been written by any number of jazz fans. It expresses certain ideas which are, I believe, shared by a great many young people today. Allow me, therefore, to address myself to them, as well as to you.

You are an earnest jazz fan, one among many; you love jazz more than anything else, but you are also capable of appreciating other forms of music (you do not say which, and that is a pity). The scope of your understanding does not, however, embrace "atonal" music, and "concrete" music seems to you the height of ridicule. As far as jazz is concerned, you are resolutely against everything which is not New Orleans. Your blacklist includes Stan Kenton and Earl Bostic, Miles Davis and Coleman Hawkins, all of whom you seem to place under the heading "bop." This strangely varied "bop" is, according to you, a degenerate form of jazz, the end result of a regrettable process of development which, if I understand you correctly, is the work of white men determined to belittle Negro art. "Technique" and "harmony" have supplanted "life." You even refuse to recognize as jazz this music in which you no longer find "the expressions of children with long lives behind them" (the image is a pretty one). "We cannot help realizing that this is no longer jazz," you specify.

Having reached this point, however, you begin to feel less sure of yourself, for it occurs to you that what you call "bop" might simply be the present state of jazz. But this would imply that, failing to understand the jazz of your day, you have taken refuge in the past. Your case would be rather similar to that of the "serious" music lover whom twenty years of Sunday concert-going have endowed with a musical culture extending from 1710 to 1910, that is from Bach's

Brandenburg Concerti to Stravinsky's *Firebird*. For this
"average music lover"—and there are thousands like him—
the rest "is not music." For you, who are an average jazz
fan weaned on the milk of Louisiana, anything which departs
from the New Orleans style "is not jazz." So saying, you
dismiss a whole body of music which you feel no need to
try to understand. You give free rein to your single-minded
taste for the jazz of the past.

Yet now another idea may occur to you. What if New
Orleans were simply a vestige, destined to survive a few
years more, until the careers of Armstrong and Bechet are
over, but no longer? Both these men are already gray-haired;
there is no reason to hope that they will still be blowing their
horns twenty years from now. What then? At this point, you
start to hedge: "Plenty of people still appreciate that music." Of course they do, but appreciation is one thing, creation quite another. To reassure yourself you tell us that jazz,
the jazz you defend, "is still alive" and you make a discreet
reference to "the rise of new musicians." Do you really
know any? What are their names? Who are the successors of
Armstrong, the descendants of Jelly Roll, the spiritual sons
of Tommy Ladnier? I, for my part, do know a few young
musicians, some of them fairly talented, who are doing their
best to revive the music of New Orleans. These disciples of
King Oliver who are perpetuating the true Negro jazz are
all white men.

This is where you begin to contradict yourself. You imply that "bop" is the disastrous result of the white man's
interference in the Negro's music; and yet it turns out that
in a few years this Negro music will exist only through the
devoted efforts of nostalgic white musicians. You accuse the
white man of having "plundered" jazz, but if I were to list
the main figures in "bop" you would find only Negroes, from

Charlie Parker to Kenny Clarke. You imagine that New Orleans jazz will last forever when, less than thirty years after its heydey, there is nothing left of it but a hollow shell. Do you really think that Bob Wilber is in a class with Bechet, that André Reweliotty can compare with Albert Nicholas, or that Mickey Larché will ever make us forget George Mitchell?

Let us pause to consider this notion of "immutability" which you bring up rather irresponsibly, I am afraid, and without having given much thought to its logical consequences. Art is the very soul of a people. If New Orleans jazz was a faithful image of the American Negro at the end of the first quarter of our century, how could this still be true? The Negro has made tremendous strides since the first World War. True, there are peoples whose music has stopped developing precisely because they belong to "arrested" civilizations. But the American Negro is growing every day, and his art is growing too, not *with* him, but *within* him, since his art is *himself*.[1] You'll "hear no talk of evolution," you say; but evolution is a law which men can elude only by reverting to the worst of all possible states: stagnation.

The young American Negro of 1953 does not live, think, or feel the way his grandfather did. You have to admit that there is no reason why he should like the same music either. You may say that the Negro's development was influenced by the white man; my reply is that this has been true ever since the first African slaves set foot on American soil. Our young Negro's grandfather was also influenced by his environment. His way of living was different from that of his grandparents before him. So was his music. Do you really think that jazz is an eternal form of music? Have you ever

---

[1] When I say "art," I mean true creation, not imitations or rehashings devoid of any real significance.

wondered how it came to be and what the white man's share in its creation was? Or let me ask you another question, and I'd like you to think a moment before you answer: are you particularly interested in African Negro music and do you spend hours on end listening to the recordings brought back by the Ogooué-Congo mission, for example?

Once we agree that jazz was born of a marriage between our Western musical culture and African Negro practices, then I do not see how you can deny it the prerogatives of any living organism: a musical form is just like a human being in that it develops, grows larger and more complex, reaches maturity, then declines and dies. It can also reproduce. You deny any fundamental identity between the old jazz and the new. This viewpoint can be defended, and I shall not attack it here, for I should have to raise the problem of the essence of jazz, which cannot be summed up in a few words. But won't you at least admit that today's jazz is a descendant of yesterday's? There is no such thing as spontaneous growth in art. The family tree of jazz reads: New Orleans, swing, bop, cool; as you can see, New Orleans is a thing of the past in any case. What you don't seem to see is that it was once the "future" of something else.

One of your reasons for refusing to accept modern jazz is that you find its techniques rather complex. "Let us maintain the simple harmonies of the New Orleans structure," you say. I am very glad to see these two words—harmony and structure—in a letter from a jazz fan, though I am not sure you have a very accurate idea of what they mean. A reference to harmony is a reference to the tonal system and the word structure implies some sort of formal organization. Now, neither the tonal system nor the formal organization derived from it were invented by the Negro; both were borrowed from the European musical language, in the context of which they had gradually developed several hundred years before. Just what do you mean by "simple harmonies"? Do you mean that only the tonic and dominant chords have a right to exist in jazz? But then why should you accept even *two* chords? As an expert in primitive jazz recently reminded us, Negroes on the plantations of nineteenth-century Louisiana improvised on *just one chord*. I could be even more dogmatic and assert that the existence of that single chord is the sign of an embryonic harmonic sense which is essentially European (the chord is an invention of the white man) and must therefore be done away with. But, you exclaim, if there are no more chords at all, if we return to the preharmonic period, what is to become of jazz? This is the point I want to make. For since we are led to acknowledge the *necessity* of a European leaven in our "purely Negroid" music, how can we then prevent that music from fermenting? Are we going to cut off jazzmen's ears? The growth of the harmonic seed in American Negro music is worth careful attention: one chord in 1875, two or three chords in 1900, several more in 1925 (the records of King Oliver already contained some of those dangerous diminished sevenths); where and when should the line be drawn? Are we going to prevent a young musician's adding a harmonic combination to his vocabulary when we have allowed the previous generation to develop theirs as they saw fit?

I hope that you will now begin to see how subjective your viewpoint is. The fact is that you want jazz to be *such that you can understand it*. If Gillespie hears a harmonious set of relationships in what sounds to you like a discord, you think it is Gillespie who is wrong. It does not occur to you that if you were more gifted, or perhaps had received a better musical education, you would be capable of having musical experiences which, for the moment, are completely beyond you. Supposing you were given an opportunity to hear good modern jazz in the company of the best Paris jazzmen: would you ascribe their reactions to the actual pleasure they derive from what they hear, or to some sort of snobbism? For I should like to point out that if your sole criterion is the pleasure that *you* derive from a given piece of music, why should you refuse to grant equal value to another piece of music which, though it may not happen to please you, does please *other people?*

But let's get back to this notion of evolution. Whenever a creative minority is responsible for a progressive development, the result is a temporary estrangement from the general public. Let us take the very simple image of a rather heavy ball attached to a rubber band. If I pull on the rubber band the ball doesn't move at first; but if I keep on pulling, the tension will increase until the ball's inertia is overcome and it starts to roll. The hand pulling on the rubber band represents the artist, of course, and the ball the general public. Thus, in moving ahead of the public, the artist also exerts a strong attraction upon it, and the public does finally catch up with him (generally when his creative powers are exhausted). This estrangement can, in some cases, last a long time. The "atonal" music which, by your own admission, you do not understand, already existed before the first World War. The experiments in modern jazz are more recent, but there again you have been left behind. The dilemma that confronts you is now becoming apparent: either you must make the effort necessary to assimilate the art of your generation or else, like the vast majority of your contemporaries, you must simply give up. This may be the solution you have already chosen; perhaps you are not equipped to be on the right side of the rubber band. Twenty-five years ago you would have been against Louis Armstrong.

Yet your opposition would not have meant that Armstrong's efforts were wasted, nor will it prevent those of today's artists from being fruitful. Your children will become accustomed to present-day art forms at an early age and will readily adopt them. But time will have passed and they will be faced with the dilemma that has faced every man since the dawn of civilization.

2

I now come to the more general question of jazz criticism. Please do not think that I am changing the subject, for no matter how unsophisticated you claim to be, your ideas reflect, consciously or unconsciously, those contained in the few books you have read. As a matter of fact, it would surprise me if you did have clear-cut, open-minded ideas on jazz. In the past twenty years, there has been far too much contradictory writing published on the subject, far too many hasty and peremptory opinions expressed. I do not mean to heap abuse on any particular critic; I have been guilty of this sort of thing myself. Your case interests me in so far as it confirms the absurdity of all dogmatic criticism. Let's examine it objectively.

One day a man sits down at a typewriter and pecks out what he regards as the definitive condemnation of modern jazz. On his sole authority a whole generation of musicians representing the tendency known as "bop" are expelled from the jazz family. A thousand miles away, in the North African countryside, a young man—yourself—discovers jazz through a few records representing a tendency which is very different and certainly much older (you mention the names of musicians born at the turn of the century). Then he happens to read the books containing the aforesaid condemnation of "bop." Some years later the young fan moves to a large city. There he hears music which, though it is called jazz, is—or seems—very different from the music he likes. He reads magazines which defend musicians whom he regards as dangerous heretics. He is outraged: "Nowadays they call jazz something which is called bop in the books I've read."

This reaction is easily understandable. Our young man's first contact with modern jazz produced, as was to be expected, an unfavorable impression.[7] Moreover, he was predisposed to adopt the conservative opinions of his favorite authors, since he already shared their enthusiasm for New Orleans. A certain inertia, combined with a rather strange, though widespread conception of music, took care of the rest.

When you had gotten over your first feeling of confusion, you were faced with two possible attitudes. The first—and most difficult—consisted in reconsidering the entire problem. You had been convinced by certain arguments, but you might have begun to wonder whether there wasn't another viewpoint upheld by even more convincing arguments. You chose, however, the second attitude: you decided that you were right in the first place and that the young jazzmen of today were wrong in the eyes of history. Why? Because you blindly followed your own tastes, and these drew you toward traditional jazz and away from modern jazz. You did not have the strength to doubt.

Nevertheless, you must be credited with "a year of fruitless efforts" after which you completely lost interest in a form of music which, according to you, "leaves a disagreeable impression of lifelessness and spinelessness. . . a feeling of unhealthy morbidity." Just what are you looking for in music? You sound like those exponents of "socialist realism" and "progressive music" who use similar terms to condemn the "bourgeois cosmopolitanism" of Western art as against the "happy, healthy" music of the Soviets.

I really cannot go along with you there. The poems of Baudelaire and Rimbaud have also been called "morbid"; I, for my part, merely find them beautiful. I confess I am stupefied whenever I hear such adjectives applied to music. If I understand you rightly, Miles Davis is to be exiled from the land of jazz because of his "morbid and unhealthy" disposition! Once again we have put our finger on the completely subjective nature of your critical standards.

But let us proceed. In your repugnance for any music that does not "laugh" or "cry" exactly according to your wishes, you go so far as to exclude Coleman Hawkins from jazz! You imply that Hawkins is a "bopper"—with all the restrictions that this word implies for you. Here you certainly step out of line and display great originality; I have never heard it said of Coleman Hawkins that he wasn't a true jazz-man. I can only congratulate you on your candor and the courage with which you lay yourself open to ridicule. Though rather unexpected to say the least, this rejection of yours does afford an opportunity to gauge the futility of the subjective criteria with which some people claim to set limits on an art form. In excluding bop from the world of jazz simply because the music of Gillespie and Parker happens to disagree with them, one wonders whether our small-time inquisitors were expecting this particular excommunication. And yet you are no less logical than they: "I like jazz; I don't like Hawkins; therefore, Hawkins is not a jazzman." This is the gist of your argument, and though completely emotional, it is no weaker than theirs. I, however, should like to know how you would react if a Bunk Johnson fan were to come along and, paraphrasing your own words, deny Louis Armstrong's music the right to be called jazz: "If one takes

Bunk as a reference—and his music came first—there is no
reason why one should go on calling Armstrong's jazz; we
can not help realizing that this is no longer jazz!" What
would be your answer to that? You may think this is pure
conjecture, but if so you're wrong. A few years ago, the
magazine *Jazz Hot* conducted a survey in which readers
were asked to name "the five greatest figures of jazz." Louis
Armstrong came out on top; he was mentioned on 97.4% of
the lists received. This meant that one out of every forty
readers did *not* regard Armstrong as one of the leading men
in jazz. I was intrigued by these figures; I wanted to know
who repudiated the man whom almost all of us regard as our
greatest classic. I was surprised to discover that only half
of these intransigent fans consistently displayed very modern
tastes in their replies; the other half swore only by Bunk
Johnson, Kid Ory, and George Lewis. You may be sure that
these people are sincere in their belief that jazz is limited to
the strict Louisiana era as it was brought to light in the "re-
vival" records. Now, perhaps, you see how risky it is to draw
dividing lines where there are no natural boundaries; one is
always in danger of being beaten at his own game by even
greater conservatives than himself.

3

Let us now examine a more general problem, one which
you dispose of rather cavalierly, I feel. If we assume that it
is permissible to talk or write about jazz, how should one do
so? In other words, should criticism be couched in lyrical,
poetical, technical, dogmatic, or philosophical terms?

The first specialized jazz critics felt that their task was to
judge and classify. With one hand they would weigh the
merits of each individual jazzman and with the other, file
him away in their catalogues. This filing system also had a

certain effect on the grades given each musician, according to the critic's personal taste: "A is probably more talented than B, but B belongs to the New Orleans school and therefore deserves a bonus for purity." We all know that this sort of thing soon leads to dogmatism; categories give way to boundary lines and black marks to excommunications.

Why is it that we younger critics, though we may have begun by imitating our elders, have since taken a very different tack? Why do we feel that the work of our forerunners was, on the whole, very harmful, even though we are indebted to them for a number of contributions without which we might not have been able to get under way at all? It is because they seem to us naive, impulsive, opinionated, hyperbolical, and, in the last analysis, rather futile. We do not like music to be discussed with a quaver in the voice; we do not like to see artists given grades like schoolboys by peremptory dogmatists. What was the use of those facile outbursts of lyricism, those value judgments and idealizations? What do I care if some self-styled oracle thinks such-and-such a musician is "terrific" or such-and-such a chorus "awful"? Either I am capable of realizing these things for myself or I am not. And if I am not, why should I go to swell the ranks of a congregation, persuading myself that the God-given word is right?

We have attempted to replace this form of criticism—which seems to have had some influence on you—with another, based upon different standards. Our primary concern is *objectivity*. Like our predecessors, we feel that an examination of a given musical phenomenon should begin with a description of it. The difference lies in our choice of methods. In the past, critics were generally content to describe the emotional state aroused in them by the music under examination. Allow me to borrow from one of our readers this excellent parody of the authors you seem to appreciate: "Toward the end there's a terrific note, not immediately after it's gone up, but almost; then it goes down into the bass again in a crazy way and after that it's really gone."[2] In this kind of criticism, the subject is often little more than a mirror in which the critic complacently gazes at his own reflection. I grant you that jazz critics are not the only ones who succumb to this temptation, as one can easily see from reading any newspaper. But this is no excuse.

It is not and cannot be the critic's role to step into the shoes of the artist in an illusory attempt to convey to readers the poetic resonance of a piece of music. If this beauty has not been experienced, the most lyrical commentary in the world can only obtain a superficial approval from the listener. This is the pitiful result generally attained by criticism based on value judgments. We, on the other hand, refuse to assume that the world revolves about our likes and dislikes. Though we often state our preferences, handing out praise or making reservations, it is merely to acquaint the reader with our attitude toward artistic phenomena, so that he may compare his viewpoint with ours, while remaining free to form his own opinion. The practice of giving "stars" is justified only on the lowest levels of criticism, such as record tips for busy readers.

How, then, is one to describe music? Merely by stating the facts as clearly as possible. On this score, it seems, our views are farther apart than ever, for I find this statement in your letter: "Let us leave musical dissection games to those who enjoy that sort of thing; fifths, sixths, sevenths and ninths, diminished, augmented, upside down or inside out, this is not music." I can understand your being dismayed

---

[2] Charles Garnier, "Impartialement parlant" (Tribune Libre), in *Jazz Hot,* June, 1948.

and even revolted by these apparently forbidding terms which no one has ever bothered to explain to you. I would like to know what sort of monsters these harmless words conjure up for you. I should point out that here again you are not alone. "When I hear someone mention a seventh," a fan once said to me, "I run." And yet if one is at all concerned with precision, one is forced to use the only exact terms which the language has to offer. It is not, I repeat, a matter of *dissecting* music but merely of describing it clearly.

When we musicians hear the name of an interval, it suggests something as familiar to us as the name of a color to a painter. Instead of referring to an ascending ninth, perhaps you would prefer me to say "it goes up." And yet precision does have its advantages. If I happen to read an article in which a "sequence of augmented fifth chords" is mentioned, I shall have a very precise notion of the musical passage referred to, and if I later have an opportunity to hear the piece containing these chords, I will be able to recognize them fairly easily when they occur. Moreover, it is possible to hold an aesthetic discussion on the basis of this precise and incontrovertible fact. I should certainly be at a loss in either of these cases had the critic merely referred to "a group of tortured harmonies" or, worse yet, made up some sort of vaguely literary—or literarily vague—phrase depicting the "metaphysical anguish" allegedly produced by these fifths.

I already know your answer to that. "Your scholarly descriptions are useless to me since I don't understand them." Unfortunately we live in a country where children are taught to distinguish between colors but not between notes. I therefore admit a priori that the young critics—at least insofar as they deal with difficult subjects—can expect to be understood by only a few readers. There is just one remedy for this: the reader who wishes to acquire a deeper knowledge of musical matters must make an effort of his own. I feel that a young man of twenty, whose passion for music is real, should not shrink from devoting a few hours of study each week to a better understanding of the mysteries of artistic creation. For the goal of intelligent criticism is to provide the music lover with a lens enabling him to magnify, as it were, the details of a work and, at times, to glimpse certain aspects of it which are partly hidden to the naked eye.

Needless to say the problem is not a simple one. Though it is possible, through analysis, to shed light on the technical mechanics of improvised music, no one has yet been able to elucidate the outward manifestations of swing; similarly, words do not seem capable of describing phenomena having to do solely with the texture of sound. These elements may simply defy analysis, though this is not absolutely certain; our intelligence should be able, in one way or another, to grasp what our sensibility has been able to feel. Man is not so compartmentalized as all that. The fact remains, however, that our methods of analyzing rhythmic and purely aural phenomena are still in their infancy. We must not forget that jazz criticism has only just emerged from childhood and must be borne with for a while.

The description of musical realities must be carried as far as may be necessary. It must be thorough, impartial, and display a maximum of intellectual honesty. This is indispensable if aesthetic meditation is to be carried out in proper perspective, for such descriptions serve to polarize meditation, by making it a direct and continual function of factual observation. Analysis enables us to ground our meditation on objective, concrete reality. This does not make meditation any easier, but it can, at least, relieve it of the gratuitous character which it so often has.[8]

Please understand me. I do not believe that genius is subject to demonstration. When I describe and comment upon one of Armstrong's or Parker's choruses, I know perfectly well that something essential will be missing from both description and comments, something which my faculties as a whole can apprehend, and without which even the most technically perfect work can never transcend certain limits. When we feel the presence of this "something," all we can do is say so, for does there even exist a genius capable of taking it as a theme of critical analysis? A great poet might be, though even Baudelaire's attempt to convey the poetic essence of Wagner's music remains unconvincing. One of the most glaring mistakes of the old-style critics was their attempt to convey the incommunicable when they were not equipped to do so. For want of any poetic genius they were reduced to homily, and floundered about ridiculously in a hodgepodge of adjectives.

I know that I have by no means exhausted the chief problems raised in your letter, but I would like to think that I have given you food for thought. I decided to step into this debate because it distresses me to see young people turn their backs on the art forms that are truly representative of their era, whether in jazz or any other field. I also felt that I had to come to the defense of criticism as I see it. You, after all, rather priggishly reduce criticism to a game for highbrows who are interested only in slaking their shameful thirst for "crossword puzzles." I hope to have rehabilitated in your esteem a form of criticism which takes pride in limiting its investigations to tangible realities, and which has the courage to keep still rather than talk nonsense, even if this discretion is interpreted as "intellectualism"; a form of criticism which does not seek to impose prefabricated views on the reader, asking not merely his adherence, but his actual participation.

Sincerely yours,

A. H.

CHAPTER 5

"Where the Last Come First..."

My dear André Hodeir,

I must tell you how much I enjoyed reading your article in the last issue of *Jazz Hot*.[9] For me the joy of reading has nothing to do with the realm of opinions, ideas, and, above all, of polemics, with which you are so concerned. The mind's enjoyment is never deceptive, whereas ideas are; they destroy the intelligence, they destroy men, and then they die. Since you have brought up this matter of intelligence, allow me to pass on to you, helter-skelter, a few of my observations. Intelligence is not quite the opposite of intellectuality, but almost. I don't mean that stupidity consists in knowing a great deal, but it is more prominent in the wise than in the humble. Remember the story of the astrologer who fell down a well. Personally I am not very disturbed by that little tragedy of mental ineptness, and my only regret is that astrologers do not fall alone: one way or another they manage to drag their contemporaries down with them.

Ernest Renan is supposed to have said that the development of his thinking rejoined, toward the end of his life, the natural, inborn philosophy of any Paris street urchin. This tribute to youth and simplicity was not without a certain coyness. He would have been rather embarrassed to wake up one morning in the skin of an anonymous little Parisian.

And yet a highly developed culture is often tantamount to a kind of transposition of naturalness to that simplicity which is so hard to attain.

We have all had our moments of enthusiasm for laboratory experiments, all the sketches and skeletons, discoveries and failures, which are so much more glorious than armchair art not to speak of a certain form of aesthetic masochism: we have our choice. Let everyone take his pleasure where he finds it, with all due deference to professors who cannot abandon their classroom manner after school; it is not the object of our affections which determines our stupidity, it is our manner of being affectionate. I'll go so far as to say that one can appreciate Guy Lombardo and J. S. Bach with equal stupidity. And Kid Ory's "stupidity" (you will appreciate that I have had jazz in mind all along) will seem nothing short of paradisiac to the least naive among us: for they are no longer impressed by either subtlety or perfection, nor by the now-common practice of borrowing harmonies from Maurice Ravel and Gabriel Fauré, nor by ballads for a dead infanta. They are not surprised by the candor of Americans who turn the *Rite of Spring* into a foxtrot, imagining that they have created something new, nor by the fact that artistic endeavors of this sort do not prevent the young musicians of France and America from vying with one another in wit, elegance, and talent, that is to say, from playing jazz. But that fat, monstrous, lovely fish that wallows about in the sauce and spatters our faces with a flick of his tail, also helps us clear our brains. Those harmonious relationships, those rippling movements from head to tail are under the constant control of an intelligence. Please take this image and play with it. You will find several possible combinations: headless tails, tailless heads, heads or tails, etc. . . . and if you and I were not in complete agreement, arguments for both of us. What more can one ask of an image?

I do not know whether the Negroes who have moved so hastily from the farm to the city are still spiritually wearing their Sunday best and seriously take Maurice Ravel for a greater musician than Big Bill Broonzy. The question is a moot one but is nevertheless constantly being raised by those who suppose that jazz arrangements directly influenced by our recent and not-so-recent symphonists—and the arrangements of these arrangements—are in a higher class than music of a barefaced, popular inspiration and speak to a more intelligent advance guard. Now naiveté consists precisely in regarding outdated harmonies and other effects which have done yeoman service for the past fifty years as novelties, whereas the discriminating man, accustomed as he is to seeing mountains bring forth mice, knows enough to applaud when he sees a mouse bring forth a mountain. Forgive this sudden shift from fish to mice; I play with images the way others play with words.

Thus it was decided once and for all that jazz had *evolved* in the space of four years, from 1926 to 1930, the way music had in the space of four hundred, whereas in fact it had merely moved from a folklore condition to a state of contamination, in keeping with the requirements of fashion. And despite the working conditions with which you are familiar and a perpetual overproduction, the history of that contamination and those fashions is glorious enough for us to call them unabashedly by name and dispense with such a feeble argument. The Negro genius invents even when it plagiarizes and keeps its purity even when it is adulterated (and adulterated music is by no means less stimulating). There is no reason why Negro musicians should be kept in ignorance of our aesthetic concerns. But what moves us the most, we who invented that good old notion of "art," that good old "modern" spirit, is not a diminished chord or a subtle orchestration, nor even the most highly organized swing, but the purity, the state of grace, I almost said the STUPIDITY, that is lacking in us.

You, my dear Hodeir are not a man to settle down in paradise. You have chosen the rigorous codes of our time and I admire you for your constant efforts to apply them unfailingly and imperturbably. You are not afraid of destroying Angels.[1]

Cordially yours,
HENRI BERNARD

MY DEAR HENRI BERNARD,

It is my turn to say that I was deeply interested in your letter. You do not often express yourself publicly and it is a pity. I greatly appreciate your turn of mind and the subtlety of your ideas, though I am not sure I always grasp their many nuances. Your prose undoubtedly contains many allusions which escape me. Nor do we always give words the same meaning. When I write "stupidity"—a word which is distinctly pejorative to my mind—you seem to read "candor." As a result, it is hard for us to "connect." Still, I do not want to forego the pleasure of conversing with you a bit, even at the risk of a slight misunderstanding. I care nothing for scholars who are only that, erudites whose erudition is a trunk that they drag about with them but which they are incapable of unlocking. You know perfectly well that I am not interested in people like that. Let's take the others, those whose minds are not only well-stocked but well-made. Do you think that any of them has been able to assimilate,

---

[1] An allusion to Pascal's pun: "Qui veut faire l'ange fait la bête."— *Trans. note.*

really *assimilate* all the riches of our civilization? Let's suppose someone has. Let's suppose that one man has managed to understand all the greatest ideas expressed in the world since Socrates, that he is perfectly attuned to the works of Michelangelo, Bach, and Dante. Do you really think that there is nothing left for him to do in Europe today, at the very moment when a two-thousand-year-old civilization is dying and, at the same time, rising from its ashes like the Phoenix? He would be deliberately blinding himself to one of the most amazing periods in history—a period which is, moreover, his own.

I am not straying so far from the point as it might seem. A man may well be stifling in this dying civilization and yet be incapable of breathing the even more rarefied atmosphere provided by the new forms of thought and sensibility; that man may find that another people brings him a "vision of the world" different from our own. Many people thus regard jazz as a Fountain of Youth. Logically enough, they feel called upon to protest against any "contamination" of their "pure magic" by the "decadent" arts of our civilization. You know perfectly well, my dear Bernard, that this is a mere illusion. Jazz was never a pure form of music. It sprang out of a conflict between two cultural traditions and has constantly had to borrow material in order to survive. Take any record of the New Orleans period. Besides an immature form of swing and "hot expressionism," what do you hear? Elements borrowed from the white man's music, and a great many of them. If it is permissible to dress up the blues in such tawdry gowns as the polka or military march, why can't they be clothed in richer finery? Precisely because it's richer? Where does one's "Sunday best" begin? The first examples of American Negro music probably involved only a single chord. In King Oliver's *Dippermouth Blues,* there are at least four different chords. How can one blame Ellington for having added still more? The seed of impurity, after all, was the *chord* itself, which did not exist in African music.

You do not seem to enjoy jazz thoroughly, my dear Bernard, other than in its folklore state. Here the gulf between us widens, for it is precisely the folk forms of jazz that move me the least. Not that I don't like the old-time blues; I simply do not find them any more attractive than many other forms of folk music, some of which I even prefer. If we are out to purge ourselves of Western art, why, let's change scenery completely, let's go to Africa or the Far East. There is not a musician worthy of the name who wouldn't give all the folk blues in the world for just one minute of the extraordinary Balinese music. If it's "purity" and a "state of grace" that you're looking for, you'll find no better example of it than in this "primitive" music in which the most critical ears have never detected the slightest Western influence; this is not true even of the earliest jazz.

You may be right; I may be a destroyer of angels; I may be insensitive to heavenly stupidity. But though a yokel's stupidity may be less shocking than a scholar's, it can be just as ugly, especially when coupled with triviality. I am very much afraid that Kid Ory achieved this formidable combination. The paradise inhabited by Kid Ory and his like is, for the moment, beyond my reach, and I confess that I do not hanker after the kind of bliss to be found in a place where the last come first and where one risks having neighbors of this sort.

Intelligence, even when it operates mainly as a negative force—as it does in bridge and in jazz, as well—is still more valuable than stupidity, even folk stupidity.

Sincerely yours,
A. H.

CHAPTER 6

Letter on the Blues, Improvisation, and the Essence

After heaping praise on my book *Jazz: Its Evolution and Essence*, are American critics now discovering that, when all is said and done, it is a purely intellectual construction, entirely unrelated to reality? This seems to be the conclusion of a debate organized by two of their most eminent representatives, Whitney Balliett and Leonard Feather.[10]

Perhaps the author may be allowed to propound, in defense of his point of view, a few arguments which may, after all, be just as valid as those set forth in this discussion by Billy Taylor. But first let me take care of two points, neither of which, I feel, are by any means negligible, since had they been settled to begin with, this discussion would probably never have been held or would, at least, have taken quite another turn. Leonard Feather and the fourth member of the panel, Nesuhi Ertegun, both have an excellent command of French. I am therefore surprised that, before attacking David Noakes's translation—which, on this particular point, seems to me above reproach—it did not occur to them to refer to the original. Would this have been doing too great an honor to the author and translator of a book which, despite the offhanded way in which one of its main conclusions has been attacked, nevertheless represents several years of effort and reflection?

It seems, moreover, that my estimable contradictors did not even take the trouble to refer to the English version. Had they done this they might not have had to so puzzle over my intentions. For not only did I write the sentence that was at the origin of their discussion: "This same piece (Hawkins's *Body and Soul*) authorizes me to disqualify, as essential characteristics, *the language and the spirit of the blues*, which play a great role in the gestation of jazz but do not seem to be *constant and necessary* elements," but immediately went on to dispel any possible misapprehension on this score: "The form of the blues is even less important than the style." And a bit further on I write: "Improvisation, whether individual or collective, is not essential either."

Three years ago, when West Coast jazz was in its heyday and when cool musicians drew their inspiration from Miles Davis's famous recording session for Capitol, no one was shocked by these assertions; now that blues have come to the fore again they may seem aggressive and unreasonable. But, my dear Whitney Balliett, don't you find it unreasonable to start a discussion on the concept of essence without first defining the term? You have to admit that I, at least, took the trouble to do so. I began the chapter entitled "The Essence" by making what I regard as a necessary distinction between the components and the essence of jazz: "We shall regard as essential only those characteristics that are at once specific and constant." To make myself clearer, I quoted a Husserlian definition coined by Lucien Malson: "The essence of a thing consists of the elements that it would be impossible to suppose absent without destroying the thing itself," and I went on to observe that "This would seem to be the only way to state the question."[11]

If you wished to cast doubts on the cogency of my assertions, you obviously should have begun by formulating the notion of essence differently. To tell the truth, I do not think that you would have succeeded in defining the problem better or more "modernly" (i.e., more in the spirit of Husserl) than Lucien Malson. Does the fact that you made no attempt to do so mean that you implicitly accept my definition of "essence"? In that case, the objections raised by Leonard Feather and yourself vanish automatically, as I shall attempt to prove; for the conclusions I reach on the basis of these premises are perfectly correct.

1. *Improvisation is not essential*

When I write that improvisation is not essential—that is, that it cannot be both specific and constant—you, my dear Leonard Feather, rise up in protest and express your "total disagreement" on this score. Will you, for a moment, allow the arranger in me to take up where the aesthetician leaves off? Don't you think that, as an arranger, I could compose an orchestral score in, let us say, a blues style, in which there would be only ensemble writing and no solos, as in the orchestral introduction to Basie's *Every Day*? Don't you think that Frank Foster, George Russel, and a dozen other first-rate arrangers could write similar pieces? Now suppose Count Basie were to make up a concert bill with these pieces and that his orchestra were to play them with all the feeling and swing that we know they can muster. Wouldn't that be an authentic jazz concert, despite the fact that it contained no solos, let alone any improvising? Is this concert really so inconceivable, Leonard? And when it was over could you still maintain that improvisation is an essential element of jazz, *essential in the Husserlian sense of the term?*

To my mind, improvisation is simply a *means of expression.* Jazz history proves how fruitful it has been, and as musicians we know how important it still is. Yet the mere fact that it is possible to play *one minute of jazz* without resorting to this means of expression, without even *referring* to it—and I use this term advisedly—suffices to show that it is not really *essential.*

2. *The blues is not essential*

Let us get on to the problem of the unessentiality of the blues which, though far more difficult to demonstrate, seems to me just as obvious. Here I intend to go against my own aesthetic convictions, for I am only concerned with objective truth, not value judgments. The fact that at the present time the blues is of vital importance *to me* will not lead me to make the mistake of Billy Taylor, who is so wrapped up in his personal tastes (or, perhaps, in his own secret failings) that he hears the blues where there simply is none.

Please let us not confuse semblance with reality, the outward form of a thing with its essence. Man's form involves two legs and two arms, but what is *essential* to man? A man with one leg can still be a man in the deepest sense of the term. Of course, a one-legged man is an imperfect man, and it is not desirable for a man to have only one leg; similarly, a jazz concert which lacks either improvisation or an element of the blues would not be a perfect jazz concert and in my opinion such a concert is not desirable. But here again we are bringing in a value judgment which can only confuse the issue.

Billy Taylor claims that Hawkins "especially has a unique

feeling for the blues which comes out in *Yesterdays, Body and Soul,* and whatever he plays." But when Leonard Feather draws the conclusion which seems to follow from this statement, suggesting that this feeling must therefore be expressed in the form of a melodic or harmonic language, Billy Taylor feels the ground give way beneath him and beats a hasty retreat: "Well, I hesitate to oversimplify in that particular case because I tend to go back to the spirit. It's not the fact that a man on certain occasions would flat a certain note, bend a note or do something which is strictly a blues-type device." Is he not admitting that I was right when I said, in substance, that the blues language is not a constant and necessary element of jazz?

For it would be very difficult indeed to find many blue notes in Hawkins's famous solo, and the cautious tone suddenly adopted by my contradictor is easy to understand. "It's just," says he, "that whatever this nebulous feeling is [nebulous indeed, considering the Taylor method of musical analysis!], the vitality they seem to get in the blues [only the blues has vitality, of course!], whatever it is makes the difference between Hawkins's *Body and Soul* and society tenor players' *Body and Soul.*" Observe Billy Taylor's splendid logic, which he already displayed in our debate on Art Tatum. "The proof that German is at the origin of Chinese," he tells us, "is that the Chinese and Russian accents have nothing in common."

But let's be serious. I, for my part, maintain that Coleman Hawkins is one of those musicians who has successfully attempted to renew jazz outside of the blues framework. These musicians have found a new "feeling," as far removed from the "society feeling" as from the "blues feeling." Certain great jazz musicians interpret ballads with the blues feeling, and you are quite right, Nesuhi Ertegun, to recall this fact in connection with Billie Holiday, but you are wrong to make it a general rule. Just listen to the improvisation on *These Foolish Things* in *The Artistry of Stan Getz* and let me know if you honestly think you can get even intermittent whiffs of the blues!

This does not mean that Hawkins and Getz are incapable of playing impeccable blues styles should the occasion arise. It so happens that most great jazz musicians are fairly all-around men; none of them is missing a leg. But there is no reason why we can't conceive of a great jazzman whose music would be entirely unrelated to either the language or the spirit of the blues. I might feel that this musician is aesthetically in the wrong—I have already said how important the blues is to me as a musician—but I would not deny him the right to exist, as Billy Taylor probably would.

If my approach to the work of the great jazzmen is correct, then the blues feeling is not both specific and constant; and this, Whitney Balliett, is why I must disagree with you and continue to think that the spirit of the blues is not, *in the Husserlian sense of the term,* essential to jazz.

CHAPTER 7

A Formidable Wager

"**I**n the last analysis, those jazzmen remain who achieve
the respect of their colleagues. Popularity polls and critics'
judgments, by contrast, tend to be transitory. (Dave Brubeck, for example.)"[1] So says Nat Hentoff in a recent article.[12]

Is it true, as my fellow-critic implies, that the critics and
even the public have no part in shaping that famous "verdict
of posterity" which we regard as an absolute value? (though
no doubt wrongly, since that verdict varies from one period
to the next). Even if we do accept it as an absolute value—
as some people do—must we look upon it as a result of a
gradual crystallization of the conscious, articulate opinions
of a handful of especially shrewd and lucid musicians endowed with immediate insight? Nat Hentoff does not make
this mistake: "The way a musician plays, rather than what
he says, will indicate which of his contemporaries and predecessors have particularly influenced him. The highest praise
a musician can give another—up to a point short of blatant
imitation—is to show by his work that he has been influenced by the other's work. (But the compliment becomes

---

[1] Nat Hentoff, "The Shaping Influences" in *Record Whirl,* July, 1956.

small unless the young musician then goes on to develop his own style.)"

In more general terms, this observation means that the great art of today necessarily engenders the art of tomorrow. At times this filiation is immediate and direct, at others it is very long in taking effect. Notions that were thought to be dead and buried have spanned the centuries and been brought up to date again in the context of new art forms whose origins are entirely different. Thus the spirit of Beethoven's late works has reappeared in the most recent serial music and Duke Ellington may well have a greater influence in the future than he has had in the past.

But we must not think that this takes care of the "verdict" aspect of our problem. Things would be far too simple if it could be reduced to a matter of percentage, as Hentoff seems to imply. A human life may simply not be long enough to provide the perspective necessary for a qualitative estimation of this percentage; in that case one is likely to fall prey to the illusion of quantity. The sight of an army of disciples is always impressive, but does one always stop to wonder where that army is going or whether it is moving at all? During the past ten years Maurice Ravel's following has been simply falling apart, and yet by percentage he was one of the most influential composers of his time. Who can claim today that this influence, though numerically tremendous, has produced any great works? In jazz, the case of Benny Goodman is similar. Around 1940 he had countless disciples, but Charlie Parker and Lester Young were not among them.

The examination of an artist's work with an eye to detecting its origins is useful only insofar as one is already convinced of the artist's merits. What do I care if such and such a musician, whom I regard as mediocre, belongs to one tendency rather than another, if he is influenced by Count

Basie rather than Dizzy Gillespie? Does the fact that there may be thousands of musicians like him prove that the Count is more important than Dizzy? If our answer is no, then we are forced to admit that the law of influences proves nothing whatever; and if we postulate that this law also favors the best musicians—which is obviously true—then we are expressing a preliminary value judgment which deprives our "law" of any significance.

2

Once we admit the necessity of a value judgment, it would seem permissible to bring the audience back into our system of references. An artist who has no audience can live only for the future, only, that is, for a future *audience*. If that audience is never found, it proves that his work has no value. An artist who is ignored by his immediate contemporaries is often in the right; but he is in the wrong if he does not find an audience sooner or later. There may have been great artists who remained unknown, but this lack of recognition, obviously unprovable, can only stem from very special circumstances, such as the destruction of a man's work or his refusal to make it public. French music lovers are beginning to appreciate row music in spite of all the barriers thrown up around it by critics, by the powers that be and even, to some extent, by row composers themselves. In the field which concerns us here, one may wonder whether music lovers are coming to modern jazz. They are, of course, but not unerringly.

And it is precisely in the terms of the public's errors that one must attack the problem. The public, I suspect, has always erred to some extent. A century ago the mass of "connoisseurs" were applauding Meyerbeer as the most representative composer of their time. Today a name like that of

Honegger is revered in the same way, yet no one seems aware of the obvious analogy. It is only fair to add, in deference of the public, that critics do not always advise them as well as they might. Often the public's errors were originally the critics'. Don't you think, Nat Hentoff, that the prestige enjoyed by Dave Brubeck is *also* the critics' fault?

But let's move one more rung up the ladder and lay the primary responsibility at the door of the real culprits; if mistakes have been made there is no doubt but what it is the musicians themselves who are guilty. Here my point of view rejoins that of Nat Hentoff but is also diametrically opposed to his. Hentoff seems to feel a priori that musicians are infallible, whereas I claim that they are as capable of making mistakes as anyone else and do so just as often. The cases of Meyerbeer and Honegger would have been inconceivable without the help of a good many musicians; I would even hazard to say that it was they who took the lead.

Musicians, and jazz musicians in particular, are contemptuous of criticism—at least they are in France. And their contempt is not limited to specialists; it embraces the very principles of criticism. Yet jazzmen themselves continually engage in criticism, for while it has long since been proven that there is almost no hope of *making a jazz musician talk,* they do talk a great deal among themselves. Throw any two of them together and they immediately begin discussing the merits of a third. Is this not criticism? It's spoken criticism, of course, but it is no less effective than, and at times fully as caustic as, the written kind; and though musicians seldom actually write criticism they supply critics with material in spite of themselves. One out of two critics— I am still speaking of France—pattern their judgments after the opinions of jazz musicians, wavering and remote as these opinions admittedly are. Criticism of this kind obviously risks going off half-cocked, for the critic rarely knows the musician well enough to have a true picture of his mind.

This spoken criticism is not without interest; I myself have known some fine examples of it. Hentoff is probably right, however, in preferring to go by the indications to be found in a musician's playing. A jazzman's musical ideas often tell more about him than his ideas per se. Sometimes, in fact, there is a contradiction between the two. Though many musicians are fond of the music that has influenced them (Guy Laffite admires Herschel Evans and Maxime Saury, Barney Bigard), the reverse is sometimes true as well; Hubert Rostaing, for example, prefers Johnny Hodges and Charlie Parker to Benny Carter and Benny Goodman, yet his playing is chiefly influenced by the last-named musicians. A jazzman, then, may be said to tip his hand completely, only when selecting his partners—provided that his choice is perfectly free. A musician who is never invited to play with his fellows is faced, independently of any personal problem, with just one alternative: either he is too far ahead of his time or else his musicianship is, to say the least, open to question. Indeed, I cannot admit the possibility of a collective error in this particular field; on the other hand, I shall take care not to give an absolute value to a musician's "score," to the number of times, that is, that his fellows have preferred him to another.

Critics and the public can only make errors of judgment, whereas the musician stands in danger of erring on several levels: in his opinions, in his choice of partners, and in his music. As we have seen in the past, the momentum of a so-called great musician can suffice to tow a whole crowd of followers along behind him. These followers, on the other hand, are not likely to be followed in turn, though it may take some time for them to realize that the movement has died out; disciples of Kid Ory still exist even today. Then too, a great many musicians demand no more of jazz than the joy of playing, the kind one can derive from chess or tennis. Still other musicians, some of them highly proficient, combine a thorough technical knowledge with an even more thorough lack of aesthetic judgment. They are the ones who are easily taken in by the apparent technical perfection of a musician's work and build the reputation of those modern Meyerbeers who have abounded in the brief history of jazz.

3

There is no reason why any one of us should not be able to express a relevant opinion about an art of the past, since we are familiar with its development as a whole and possess many points of reference. On the other hand, only the musicians themselves—and in fact only the most clear-sighted among them—can appreciate the meaning and importance of the different aspects of today's production. To avoid being badly mistaken about a present-day work one must be caught in the contemporary current oneself; one must not be working up some blind alley but have a keen, deep awareness of the actual situation as it develops from month to month and from week to week. This being the case, it should be easy to understand that only musicians can be "in the swim," and only a minority of them at that.

The observer must have a point of reference within himself, some sort of personal conviction to serve as a gauge by which to measure the achievements of others. It then becomes possible to see where a given conception is leading, to distinguish between what is valid in that conception and what is extraneous, between what is merely experimental and what is aesthetically successful. For an unevenly gifted artist can give impetus to a movement which his imperfect

works only foreshadow. An artist's effort may be truly inspired and yet the results be uninspired. Witness Varese,
Calder, Kandinsky or, in the field of jazz, Fletcher Henderson or Thelonious Monk.[13]

Only a musician armed with deep-rooted aesthetic convictions can possibly make use of the discoveries of a man
like Monk. It matters little whether or not this conviction is
easily articulated, whether or not its possessor is aware of its
historical origins; these are the critics' business. The important thing is that he be able to strip away the husk of
failures and assimilate the kernel of his forerunner's attempt. Bud Powell has done this with Monk; who will be
Tatum's Bud Powell?

One may object that his personal conviction, though it
may be our only guide through the labyrinth of present-day
art, is liable to make us overly subjective. Are we not likely
to condemn anything which is not moving in our direction?
This is where the artist is forced to lay a formidable wager,
for the soundness of his judgments depends upon the valid-
ity of his art. His opinions will be valid only if his music is.
Aside from the inherent nobleness of such a wager, its apparent subjectivity does not preclude a degree of objectivity,
for only artists can approve or condemn on good grounds.
But when I say "artists," I mean just that, and not a vague
majority defined in terms of even the most overwhelming
percentages.

Some may unjustly feel that this is to advocate a form of
shortsighted egotism. The true artist, however, does not
wear blinkers; he has, on the contrary, many pairs of eyes
to capture the myriad images of a world which, like the
artist himself, is constantly evolving. The critic who adopts
a system of references, the center of which necessarily lies
outside of himself, is in a more difficult situation. He is likely

to be accused of dogmatism, and perhaps rightly so. Would this be too high a price to pay for his rejection of eclecticism? Just as a musician who cannot find his proper path soon reaches a standstill, so a critic who approves of any undertaking whatsoever must constantly practice a kind of leveling which deprives his writings of any real persoective. Let us therefore stake our wagers on just one form of jazz—and I may add, for the benefit of my fellow musicians, that this holds true even if that form is the one which is closest to your personal conceptions. You mustn't be afraid of being right.

Part Three

On Group Relations

CHAPTER 8

Environment

When, in the course of the last decade, Duke Ellington's main soloists left him, it soon became evident that his orchestra's great period was finished.[14] The departures of Cootie Williams, Rex Stewart, Bigard, and Hodges, the deaths of Blanton and Tricky Sam each opened a fresh breach which could not be filled. It took longer for us to realize that in leaving Ellington, to all intents and purposes, Cootie, Rex, Bigard, and Hodges had put an end to their own creative activities.

Yet this was what most of their subsequent records revealed. Our first disappointment came in 1947; it was supplied by Rex. Ten concerts and twenty records showed us that the sterling horn blower of *A Portrait of Bert Williams* had turned into a second-rate clown. Next it was Bigard's turn; the dazzling musician of *Across the Track Blues* now seemed bored to death by what he was playing; unable to discard a handful of stock recipes, he could only go around in circles like a mill horse. A bit later, Hodges came too. He still had some talent left, but often his fascinating charm affected only the bleary-eyed young ladies who swoon when they hear Nat King Cole. As for Cootie, he has not yet come to Paris. This may be why we like to imagine him as great as ever. A number of relatively recent records, however, incline me to feel he would disappoint us as much—if not more—than his former partners.

There has been a great deal written about the decline of these four musicians. Most critics have set it down to age and it certainly is true that age constitutes an enormous handicap for a jazz musician. As his physical capacities diminish it becomes more and more difficult for him to express himself. A further, and very important, factor in this change is undoubtedly a slowing of the body's rhythm (the "inner time" or "real time" referred to by Alexis Carrel is necessarily of greater importance in artistic creation than physical time). A final factor involved here is a psychological phenomenon we might call the *tedium of repetition.* Any artist who does not renew his style is bound to start repeating himself, and very few jazzmen over thirty have found a fresh approach to their music. The combined result of these three factors is almost always a considerable decrease in the musician's *desire to play.* I am beginning to reach an age where I can observe this phenomenon among some of my fellow jazzmen; when it comes to improvising, they now seem reluctant and even wary, whereas at the age of twenty they were hungry for improvisation and fairly pounced on their choruses.

So we see that the age factor is a valid argument. I do not believe, however, that it provides a full explanation in the case of these four musicians. Another factor must be taken into consideration, one which seems to me equally important if not more so, and that is the musician's environment.

Jazz is a collective art; it is therefore normal that the artist should be affected by his environment, especially if he is given to improvising. The jazz band is a society in miniature whose members must get along with one another on two different levels: that of human relations and that of purely musical relations. The last-named is certainly the more important of the two. On the whole, it is better for two jazzmen who are to play together to have musical affinities rather than strictly personal ones. Yet personal sympathy is necessary, not only to hold a band together for any length of time, but also to make it "live" in the strongest sense of the term. I do not believe that a drummer can go all out in support of a soloist, nor that the soloist in question can do *his* best if the two men are mortal enemies. A few years ago we had a very promising band right here in Paris which never amounted to anything precisely because it was split up into at least two feuding cliques.

It would be a waste of time to carp about this Dostoevskian situation. I should like to think that it was exceptional, but am inclined to doubt it. The musicians themselves are more directly concerned with the problems of *musical* relation involved in this fascinating subject of environment. There have been examples of perfect harmony between two musicians; I need only cite the team of Parker and Roach. But it is easier, and perhaps more profitable, to reverse the problem and examine a case of musical friction. At the last Jazz at the Philharmonic concert we heard Benny Carter accompanied by Oscar Peterson. Now these are two fine jazzmen, both excellent musicians, but who belong to two different eras. Each has a definite conception of jazz, which his partner couldn't possibly share; in actual practice these two conceptions, though perfectly coherent in themselves, conflict on various points, and especially with regard to the harmonic system. All that came of their collaboration was that each clung to his own ideas, and the over-all impression produced was quite incoherent.

This part of the program generally gave rise to unkind criticism, but the name of the musician criticized depended on who was speaking. Some said that Carter was "old hat," but this was an unfair reproach. Carter was playing with more advanced musicians than himself, and his obvious efforts to adapt himself to their harmonic language deserved real praise. He was only partly successful, but who can blame him for that? It is not at all surprising that a musician of his generation should have difficulty placing—or even hearing—passing chords which came into use long after he had reached maturity. It merely confirms what we already knew: that it is almost impossible for a jazzman in his forties to overtake the younger generation.

On the other hand those who are systematically opposed to young jazzmen lay all the blame on good old Oscar's shoulders, fortunately very broad. According to them it was his business to place himself at Carter's disposal, since an accompanist's only duty is to be the soloist's devoted guide. Like many "common sense" notions, this one is misleading. It reflects a highly oversimplified approach to jazz, which consists in hearing not an over-all synthesis but merely a set of pieces composed of a central subject—the solo—and an accompanying background. Yet how can a collective work be valid if its various components are not thoroughly blended? The only way for Peterson to have achieved this blend would have been to repudiate his own ideas; can we blame him for having refused to do so? Could he have done so even if he had wished to? Under the circumstances, the sole responsibility for the mediocre performance of the team Carter and Peterson belongs to the man who brought them together, deliberately neglecting that indispensable unity of conception for the sake of publicity: I am referring to Norman Granz.

Examples of this sort are not infrequent. They occur whenever circumstances or a manager's insistence brings together two or more musicians of diverging tendencies. Some musicians can adjust themselves to their environment; others cannot. I remember having watched a once famous trumpet player rehearsing with an excellent pianist who was fifteen years his junior. The older man couldn't make head nor tail of the changes that his partner would reel off imperturbably. "Play me an E flat seventh," he begged. . . and the younger man sounded an E flat seventh with a sumptuous F major on top of it. "But I want an E flat seventh" the other man screamed, and the pianist hit another pair of superposed chords: E flat 7—C major, or E flat 7—F sharp minor. It was obvious that the older man simply didn't understand the chord cluster, and he went on begging for his E flat seventh. What with his untrained ear and the younger man's stubbornness, one may imagine what sort of music came out of such a "relaxed" atmosphere.

Here again, systematic opponents of modern jazz will defend the older man against the younger and extoll the virtues of recipes used in the twenties and thirties as against more recent innovations. This would logically lead to banning all but a very limited number of harmonic combinations from jazz and hence to condemning some of Ellington's most important works, which contained extremely dissonant chord groups, or Hawkins's *Body and Soul,* which is full of passing chords. It would then be necessary to establish once and for all the harmonic boundaries of jazz and decree that the presence of a ninth chord, for example, would suffice to eliminate *ipso facto* a given piece from the world of jazz. A limitation of this kind would have its absurd logic. It would certainly be more logical than the arbitrary dictates of those conservatives who claim the right to bind young musicians in chains which have long since been broken. But it will still seem absurd to anyone who believes that jazz has no harmonic essence and that it is capable of absorbing every technique —modal, tonal, polytonal, or even atonal—if it has not already done so.

Unity of outlook is just as important in the rhythm section. On the level of the orchestra as a whole, even the finest modern rhythm section would be incapable of properly adjusting to the style of the New Orleans soloists, and vice versa. The mere presence in the orchestra of another soloist of a different tendency can suffice to put a soloist "out of gear," independently of any influence on the rhythm section. Similarly, the presence of a first-rate soloist whose music is in his own spirit, will always stimulate a good jazzman. It follows from these truisms that Hodges could not help declining in his last years with Ellington (1948 to 1950); the orchestra had lost all other major soloists, its conceptions were moving further and further away from those of Hodges and its arrangements were growing worse each year.

For in my opinion the arrangement is a major "environment" factor in large and middle-sized groups. A soloist who is lucky enough to belong to an ensemble supplied by a first-rate arranger enjoys an inestimable advantage from the very start. Cootie, Rex, and Bigard left Ellington at a time when his repertory was richer than that of any other orchestra. For years they had been improvising in unique surroundings; they had been playing the loveliest arrangements of their day, and had even helped to create them. In leaving the Ellington workshop, they could only return to run-of-the-mill jazz. When deprived of the incomparable environment of Ellington's orchestra, they soon lost interest in playing. Hodges was less hard hit than the others simply because he did not undergo such a sudden change; he was the last to leave the Duke and one may safely say that he had already been bored for months when he finally decided to go.

The problem is similar in modern jazz; though today's orchestral forms are proving very difficult to elaborate, they are far more complex than those of the past. The richer the orchestral language, the more vital it is that arranger and performer see eye to eye, both emotionally and intellectually. This is theoretically possible, of course, but in practice it is extremely difficult. The arranger is generally more inclined to reflection than the instrumentalist and may thus devise abstract conceptions which the performer cannot put into concrete terms. Before the war, arrangers were already writing backgrounds which though harmonically attractive, made things very difficult for the improviser. A great many bad choruses unquestionably stemmed from backgrounds which the soloists for whom they were written had difficulty in "digesting." These attempts, though for the most part unsuccessful, did favor the development of harmonic structures and, indirectly, of melody.

The same is true today. The latest achievements in orchestration do not seem to have been completely assimilated by instrumentalists as yet. The structural complexities devised by certain arrangers sometimes place today's soloist in an even more difficult position than his predecessors of the late thirties. The resulting imbalance is, to all appearances, only temporary. However, it would seem that from now on a soloist playing with a large or middle-sized band will have to learn each arrangement by heart. If he is willing to do this, then I think that a good arrangement can, as in Ellington's heyday, give rise to a good solo, and in any case a combination of the two will undoubtedly produce very interesting results.

Then too, it often happens that a soloist who has managed

to bring off a well written but difficult statement is hardly in condition to improvise his chorus satisfactorily. He ought to have a feeling of exhilaration and musical plenitude; instead he is still tense from the difficulties he has just had to overcome and anxious about the difficulties ahead. For this reason the arranger, though he must not be content with worn recipes, must also avoid making too great a demand on his musicians. A happy medium must be found, though of course if one element has to be sacrificed, it had best be the musician's comfort. This is the only attitude that can favor the developments we are waiting for.

Will these developments produce a new form of group creation, in which the arranger will act as both engineer and captain of industry, but in which the musicians will be much more than mere workmen? Will it again be possible to conceive of the jazz band as a single unit? I hope so, for a good band presided over by a single mind is worth more than the most brilliant jam session which can be spoiled by a single ill-assorted element.

CHAPTER 9

Freedom and Its Limitations in Improvisation and Composition

T here they are, four or five musicians in shirt-sleeves.[1] It hardly matters where—a crowded night club, or an empty one, a spacious apartment on the Champs Élysées or a Park Avenue penthouse. The instruments are all that really count; let's say there are drums, bass, piano, tenor sax and trumpet.[15]

Before the first down-beat, there must be a short conference to decide, first the theme on which to improvise, and then the key and tempo. As a rule there is little discussion about the key; it is generally agreed that *What Is This Thing Called Love* should be played in C, while Charlie Parker's memorable paraphrases have made it unthinkable to take *Embraceable You* in any key but F. It is sometimes harder to decide on the tempo. The trumpet player's conception of a piece may differ slightly from the saxophonist's, and he may therefore favor a faster tempo.

When all are agreed at last, they attack the first bar. The trumpet will begin by stating the theme of *Jordu* (a "medium tempo" is always chosen for a warm-up); the saxophone may weave a countermelody, attempt to sketch in a second part in rhythmic unison or bravely choose to play the theme in octave unison. Soon the thirty-two bar statement is over and it is time to get down to business. A brief exchange of glances has shown that the saxophonist is more willing—or anxious—to play than his partner, so the trumpet player gives him the go-ahead, reserving the right to play, later on, as many choruses as his partner is about to play now. For the moment he sits back and listens, appreciating the other man's inventions, sharing his excitement if the tension rises. He knows that he will benefit by the climate that the saxophonist is creating now. The three-man rhythm section is actively collaborating in this disclosure of an immediate musical truth. Eyes shut, they are more intent on what they hear than on what they are playing. Each trusts to his own reflexes to rise instantly to the occasion if one or the other of his partners should fling him the challenge that will allow him to surpass himself and climb for a few seconds, perhaps, to the highest spheres of jazz. Later, after the trumpet solo, the pianist will have a few choruses to himself, the bass player may follow suit; then the "horns" will probably invite the drummer to share a chorus or two with them, in four bar sequences, before they return to a final statement of the theme.

Time out for a breather, then someone will suggest another number. In which key? In this tempo? Or this one? One! Two! and no sooner has the curtain fallen on the first act of this drama, farce, tragedy, call it what you will, than it has already risen on the second.

For the moment there are only five actors on stage, but a sixth may arrive at any moment, a saxophonist, a trombonist, or perhaps a guitarist. If he is respected by those who started the jam session he will be received with open arms; if not, he will be given to understand, more or less politely, that he has come to the wrong place. For indeed, the success of a jam session requires a whole set of favorable circumstances. Unless there is a certain stylistic and spiritual fellowship, a feeling of uneasy restraint will soon come over the musicians, gradually paralysing all creative effort. True, Lionel Hampton and Lee Konitz once managed to reach a *modus vivendi,* but this is an extremely rare example. Very often the mere presence of a musician—even one of recognized talent—whose notions are not absolutely geared to those of his partners, is enough to take away their desire to play, and this desire is undoubtedly the key to any achievement, big or little, in this form which is at once so easy and so difficult.

The musicians who meet for a jam session usually form a very homogeneous group; but occasionally musicians who have never met before manage to blend admirably from the very outset. The little orchestras that play, one after another, in certain Harlem clubs are often incomplete; sometimes a bass player or a drummer who comes to fill in for the night doesn't know his partners at all. Sometimes, though the occurrence is relatively rare, this hybrid composition of the orchestra will not even be noticeable.

This high degree of homogeneity necessarily stems from a very powerful tradition. These young men are all deeply influenced by the great modern jazzmen (and especially Parker), just as their predecessors were influenced by Armstrong, Basie, Goodman, Hampton, and other musicians of the swing era. This common heritage first becomes apparent in the repertory of their jam sessions. Just as, fifteen years ago, young tenor players were partial to *Body and Soul* if they were among the last disciples of Hawkins, or to *Lester Leaps In* if they had been drawn by Lester's charm to the newborn "cool" jazz, so too the jammers of today meet to play *Now's the Time, Bag's Groove, Walkin'*, or *Jordu* because they came to jazz through Charlie Parker, Milt Jackson, Miles Davis, and Clifford Brown.

The tunes that most often recur in jam sessions belong to the blues family or are AABA standards, because theirs are the simplest structures. When the tempo is slow, a ballad of an outwardly more complex structure may be chosen, but then a slow tempo in a jam session is, in itself, rather exceptional. Pure improvisation requires utmost freedom, and the widest possible field of action; any harmonic complexity constitutes a restraint. When Django Reinhardt was working with his quintet he liked to play fairly difficult themes, but when he happened to take part in a jam session he always asked for that simplest of all "16 plus 16," the A flat chorus from *Tiger Rag*.

In jazz—and especially in a jam session—the chorus, composed of either twelve or thirty-two bars, is the common frame of reference. It constitutes a perfectly circular, never-changing path. The twelve bar blues chorus forms a closed, endless circuit (Fig.1).

If we consider only the harmonic structure of the theme, each complete circuit brings us back to the starting point. The next time around the same itinerary will, structurally speaking, bring about the same sequence of events. This formal restriction was probably the source of some of the most important contributions to jazz, especially that of improvisation. Of course, the pioneers of jazz did play pieces involving two or three themes, but even so the monotony of the form must have begun to tell when they had passed the same point for the fifth or the tenth time in succession. This

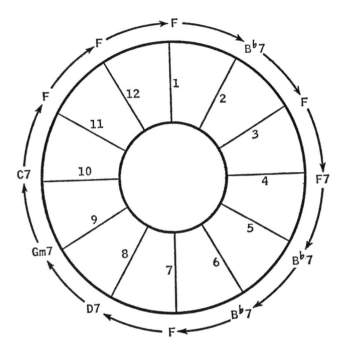

Fig. 1

was how they came to invent embellishments and, later, variations. The jazzman's effort to express himself has led him to rebel against restrictions since the earliest days of jazz. Improvisation, very limited until the early twenties, first came into its own with Louis Armstrong; twenty years later it received a new lease on life from Charlie Parker. But the freedom afforded by improvisation had to be paid for, so to speak, by a restriction in the choice of material; this may be why the blues has become the ground on which musicians usually prefer to match their skill. Before he joined the J. J. Johnson Quintet, Bobby Jaspar used to favor the widest possible repertory in a jam session; now, however, he admits that a repertory consisting of sixty per cent blues constitutes a challenge to the improviser which can, in the last analysis, prove even more fruitful. Here is another case in which freedom results from a choice and contains its own implicit limits.

This freedom has been won by soloist and accompanist alike. Today an accompanying pianist is not obliged to respect the harmonic sequence of a theme as rigidly as in the past; and if his name is Thelonious Monk, he may even extrapolate boldly on the given framework. A few points of reference, however, are still necessary; whichever road one follows from the tonic F to the sub-dominant B flat, the latter must always come at the beginning of the fifth bar of the blues; similarly, the re-entry of the tonic on the eleventh bar is still deemed indispensable. But between these two points of support the harmony may weave back and forth in an exciting game of hide-and-seek with melody.

Recently, there have been powerful attempts to emancipate even the tempo.[1] Originally this dimension was expressed by the rhythm section as a whole; later it was divided up, so to speak, among the bass (the beat), the cymbals (anacrustic expression of the beat), piano, and drums (syncopated variations around the beat). Today, however, we may be heading toward a rhythm section in which all the lines will be syncopated, so that the beat is never really expressed, but merely felt. It is too soon to be absolutely certain of this, but one thing is sure: the rhyth-

---

[1] Cf. "Les Deux Jones" in *Jazz Hot*, April, 1958.

mic language of the future is being forged in the framework of the jam session and even more in its derivative, the small improvising group.

The small improvising group differs from the jam session by a better controlled interior organization and by the fact that, in any case, it is subject to the group-leader's powers of coordination. Not that he imposes a military discipline on his fellows; discipline is never very strict in a jazz band, let alone in small ensembles. Still, it is the leader who makes the important decisions. It isn't hard for us to visualize Fats Waller arriving in a studio to cut four record sides with his "Rhythm." Of the four pieces to be done, two would be "standards," supposedly familiar to everyone, while the other two would be new tunes. This would be the first, and perhaps the last time that they would be improvised upon. The bandleader would hastily jot down the essential elements—melody and "changes." Each musician would copy them out or learn them by heart. Now there would remain only the decision on the tempo and the layout of the piece. Its length would be determined by the length of the record side (this limitation has vanished with the coming of tape); there would be three choruses, or rather two and a half (the first sixteen bars of the third variation being omitted). After a four bar solo introduction, the piano would state the melody; next the tenor would improvise the first half of a chorus, the trumpet the second half and the sixteen bar finale would be given over to a group improvisation in which trumpet, clarinet, and piano would join in a friendly struggle which would help to raise the tension. After a trial run, in the course of which the guitarist may have forgotten the harmonic figuring of the bridge, making necessary a last-minute verification, the musicians would say they were ready to record.

Disregarding the question of duration, there is very little

difference between Waller's approach and that of a modern bandleader like Horace Silver, recording *Blue Silver* or *Shoutin' Out* with his quintet. In this type of combo the arrangements are almost never written out, for they amount to very little: a few conventions, sometimes a thematic statement to be played in unison or harmonized, and a prepared coda or introduction. This kind of group has no need of long rehearsals, except to try out new members; its strength lies in the musicians' understanding of one another and the pleasure they derive from playing together.

One can imagine a good many intermediate stages between this small improvising group, whose members are closely united by long experience playing together, and the true jam session in which the participants sometimes hardly know one another. There is, for example, the "prepared jam-session," so-called because the musicians involved form a well-defined group and because the music displays structural qualities usually lacking in the true jam session. Here the musicians use introductions and codas that have become traditional with them. Most of the so-called blowing sessions ("just come and blow") recorded during the past few years belong to this category, which has produced some of the greatest masterpieces of jazz, like Miles Davis's famous *Bag's Groove* with Thelonious Monk, Milt Jackson, Percy Heath, and Kenny Clarke.

2

As soon as we reach the arrangement stage, the band's character changes; its music involves a balance between writing and improvisation which may be variously conceived. Only recently in the history of jazz have arrangers been given a chance to work with the smallest ensembles (quintets, quartets, and even trios). In the music of the Jimmy

Giuffre Three or the Modern Jazz Quartet, arrangements are at least as important as improvising. Here the leader is generally the arranger as well; he thus assumes full responsibility for the collective work, since he not only chooses his musicians, but shapes their creative imaginations in the image of his own. For an arrangement is not meant merely to afford a contrast between organized ensemble work and improvised solos; it introduces and conditions the solo, "boosting" the musician into his chorus with redoubled strength, acting, at times, as a compelling challenge.

Here we stand on the borderline between two worlds: on the one hand lie the oral traditions of music with their age-old truths; on the other, that stupendous invention of the Occident, musical composition. Is any form of music but jazz capable of making the most of both spur-of-the-moment intensity and meditative profundity? Having made this startling marriage possible may be jazz's greatest claim to fame.

The "head arrangements" used in jazz since the New Orleans era also belong to an oral tradition. In the form of a simple melodic variation, generally in rhythmic unison, this type of arrangement usually does no more than provide a harmonic coating for a melodic and rhythmic idea. Before the war a number of big bands, among them Count Basie's, developed a system of head arrangements in which each section made fairly autonomous contributions to a spontaneous "polyphony of riffs." The first trumpet would blow a riff that was immediately taken up and harmonized by the other members of his section, while trombones and saxophones devised countermelodies to the main riff. Unfortunately, this practice is dying out.

A similar technique is still used by a good many arrangers, especially those who work in the "Basie tradition." Ernie

Wilkins's famous arrangement of *Every Day* constitutes the written stylization of a method of group improvisation which might easily have developed without the help of written music as such. On the other hand, Duke Ellington's orchestra conceptions, which have influenced most modern arrangers, imply an exploration of *form* (considered as a new musical dimension) requiring a complex articulation of musical language obtainable only in the written score.

At this point we may suggest a summary classification of creative jazzmen: on the one hand stands the improvisor, and on the other a set of three separate callings which are by no means complementary: the tune writer[2] (Fats Waller), the arranger (Ernie Wilkins), and the composer (Duke Ellington). The arranger differs from the composer not so much because he works with other people's ideas but because of the more complex, formal nature of an original composition. One need only compare Ellington's *Ko-Ko* with Wilkins's and Basie's *Every Day* to see how obvious this distinction can be. (Needless to say, the dividing line is not always so sharp.)

In a jam session the themes and the musicians' creative personalities are the only elements which exist prior to the music itself. Chance and circumstances will both take a hand in the actual elaboration of the piece. In a jazz arrangement or composition, the arranger introduces a certain framework which controls and channels the performance. In modern jazz the arrangement may be defined as a *means of conditioning the soloist*. The scored passages preceding his im-

---

[2] A further distinction may be necessary on the level of the theme. Certain themes are tunes, while others are merely structures. Gershwin's *Embraceable You,* for example, may be regarded as the work of a tunewriter, whereas Monk's *Criss-Cross* is more accurately described as that of a *theme writer*. It is this term which I shall employ in dealing with his work (cf. Chapter 16).

provisation and the backgrounds sustaining it serve both to embellish and restrain it. At times they may carry him higher than he could have gone alone; they also constitute a restriction for him, but it must be understood that this very restriction can carry him higher still. Here, too, the music's definitive complexion is unpredictable; it may even vary from one performance to the next. Yet chance plays a lesser role here than in the jam session, or rather a more advanced use is made of chance by "controlling" it, as Calder does in his mobiles, or Boulez and Stockhausen do in their compositions which offer the performer a choice of "itineraries." Caught as he is between the vagaries of chance, the impulses of his ego, and the barriers placed about him by the arranger, the soloist is obliged to express himself with greater rigor.

The more thoroughly a work is *composed*, the richer its language and the more complex its form, the closer must be the contact between composer and performers; otherwise the music is in danger of losing its identity as jazz. The "classical" composer can still afford not to know who is going to play his music; this attitude is out of the question for the true jazz composer. It would be unthinkable for an arranger to have a piece played by Duke Ellington's band when it was originally written for Count Basie's. And, in fact it is almost as unthinkable to entrust a given band with a score written "in the abstract." As Duke Ellington used to say in substance: "You should know how your soloist plays poker." A composer writing for the Modern Jazz Quartet, at the moment of conceiving a phrase for Milt Jackson, should *be* Milt Jackson, or at least be able to visualize the posture he would strike while playing that phrase, the way he would screw up his mouth or bend his torso, and the angle his mallet would form with the vibraphone's keyboard.

This being the case, one can easily see what an advantage the composer has if he is also a bandleader. The reason why Ellington's music was finer than that of any other jazz ensemble to date was the extraordinary homogeneity of a band whose personnel remained practically unchanged throughout the thirties. It was as though the same blood ran in the veins of every member of that band; they had become capable of *collective creation* in the strongest sense of the term. The hapless arranger who submits a new piece to a bandleader, without knowing whether it will even be played or not, is in a completely different situation. Even if he knows the various band members well enough to have avoided the cardinal sin of miscasting a soloist, his chances of hearing his work in all its beauty are slim indeed. If his score calls for "massive phrasing" in which each man must submerge his personality (as in the ensemble sections of Frank Foster's arrangement of *Shiny Stockings* for Basie), the musicians are likely to lose interest in his piece and become "swinging robots"; if he has written a solo for someone, he may not have time to make him aware of its implications and fail to arouse in him the necessary creative attitude. Whichever the case, rehearsals will be tiresome and the performance disappointing.

Because of this intimate connection between the man who writes the music and the man who plays it, because, too, of the importance that a given attack or sonority can assume, execution remains a vital factor in the art of jazz. However, the sudden incursion of the arranger and composer into a universe once reserved for improvisers has introduced a new factor which has transformed that universe. The arrangement brings in a supplementary form of beauty, a fresh aesthetic evidence. For while it has been proven that even the loveliest arrangement, badly played, can only produce bad jazz, it is no less certain that a bad arrangement, either because of the discomfort it will cause even the best musicians or because of its intrinsic ugliness or vulgarity, in the last analysis, will result in equally bad jazz. On the other hand, very great things may be expected of the collaboration of a great arranger with a group of first-rate jazzmen, provided they are able to place themselves entirely at his disposal—and vice versa.

A collaboration of this kind might be expected to enable jazz to go beyond certain limits for the first time in its history. While the composer would enable the group to keep in touch with the splendors of form, the group's immediate aid would provide the composer with an opportunity of recording, at the appropriate moment, and in all its beauty, music which, unlike classical music, does not enjoy the privilege of being played from one generation to the next. This type of relationship, similar to that which exists between the author-director of a film on the one hand and his actors and crew on the other, might well give rise, through successive recordings (feasible until young musicians no longer "feel" the piece in question), to a type of work which though less monolithic than a film, would nevertheless display a more rigorous formal perfection than the work of jazz as it now stands. This, perhaps, is the key to a true balance between freedom and restraint in jazz.

Part Four

On Works

CHAPTER 10

The Count Basie Riddle

A great deal has been written about Count Basie's band, but much less about the Count's exceptional gifts as a pianist.[16] Though critics generally acknowledge his merits at the keyboard, they have not, until now, shown much concern for the particularities of his style, its apparent simplicity which seems, paradoxically enough, to defy analysis. It quickly became a commonplace to say that "Basie doesn't play like other pianists." Some also wondered why. Did he wish to make himself conspicuous, or was it simply a matter of concealing his technical deficiencies? As an individual he does not seem the least bit eccentric, however, and as a pianist he has had a few opportunities to prove that he is skilled enough to play differently if only he felt like it. The truth is that no one has ever supplied a satisfactory solution to what we are forced to call the "Count Basie riddle." But perhaps a thorough study of his piano music would enable us to find it.

1

The first impression gleaned from a rapid survey of Basie's records is one of extreme melodic monotony. This is partly because most of the themes he chooses are blues, but that would not be an adequate explanation if Basie handled the blues as broad-mindedly as Hines in his *Blues in Thirds* or John Lewis in *Parker's Mood*. His is a strictly traditional approach however, and often leads him to make repeated use of melodic figures which are already worn to the bone. This respect for blue notes and the triplet phrasing typical of the slow blues, as well as a nostalgia for the old boogie-woogie pianists are common traits among jazzmen of the classical era, but Basie carries them unusually far. Three-fourths of his recorded solos are so trivial from a melodic standpoint that one is tempted to wonder whether this is not intentional.

Indeed, it may be that Basie confines himself to blues out of disdain for melody per se. His approach to "standards," for example, is generally quite literal. Let's look at a few of his statements of well-known tunes. The melody of *I Never Knew* is enhanced only by the remarkable quality of Basie's touch; in *Sugar* the timid introduction of a countermelody does not for an instant take our minds off the theme; only in *Harvest Moon,* perhaps, does he attempt to vary the melody at all, using a technique rather similar to Waller's. And yet *Blue and Sentimental* proves that Basie is capable of inventing a highly original melodic phrase. As a matter of fact this is the only "colored" solo of his that I know; almost all of the rest of his piano work is "in black and white." Does this mean that he has little melodic imagination or does he simply despise melody altogether?

Basie's work is full of melodic clichés. There is hardly a record of his which doesn't contain the set figures of the old blues musicians and the typical phrases of the swing era. Here the examples are legion, from *My Buddy* and *Oh! Red* to *The Fives* and *Saint Louis Boogie*, or from *Way Back Blues* and *How Long Blues*[1] to *Boogie-woogie* and *Fare the Honey*. Far more interesting, of course, are those solos which

---

[1] Brunswick version.

display a genuine economy of melody, almost to the point of eliminating it entirely: *Bugle Blues* (second solo), *Basie Blues*, and *Red Wagon*. Later we shall see how one may interpret this startling rejection of melody. It is also interesting to note the recurrent—and apparently inevitable—left-hand cadence with which he ends a fair portion of his blues choruses in medium and in fast tempos; it turns up as often as three or four times on a single record side (*Dupres Blues, Dirty Dozens, Oh! Red,* etc.).

Yet one might have thought that Basie's need to develop his sense of melodic invention would be greater than most pianists'; he was, after all, the first "one-armed" pianist in the history of jazz. At a time when the "orchestral" approach to the piano was predominant (with Fats Waller, Teddy Wilson, and Art Tatum) Basie reconsidered the aesthetics of his instrument in a totally different perspective (in this connection, we know how great an influence he had on the subsequent generation of pianists). The musical interest of his playing is almost always concentrated in the right hand. The style is sober and unadorned, except for static groups of short, rapid notes and frequent appoggiatura-acciaccatura (in *How Long Blues*,[2] *Dirty Dozens,* etc.), generally involving blue notes. More sparing use is made of the "tremolo vibrato" technique dear to the hearts of Wilson, Hines, and their followers (i.e., *Good Morning Blues*) or of long trills replacing held vibratos (i.e., *Swingin' the Blues*[3]). Each phrase is reduced to its simplest expression: a few single notes with the occasional insertion of an isolated chord. He sometimes uses hurried rhythm effects à la Teddy Wilson (*I Never Knew*), or a system of successive—or alternate—

---

[2] Columbia version.
[3] Victor version.

thirds borrowed from Fats (*I Never Knew, Doggin' Around, Farewell Blues*).

The left hand is often completely silent and becomes prominent only for special disrupting effects like the syncopated chord which cuts brusquely into the melody of his solo in *Oh! Red*. On the whole it is extremely discreet. Basie relies on the rhythm section to keep the tempo, and it is in this sense that he has been called a "one-armed pianist." The copious accompaniment of tenths in *Sugar Blues*—reminiscent of Waller's *Keepin' Out of Mischief Now*—or the varied patterns used in *Café Society Blues* are very exceptional. The rest of the time Basie's left hand merely provides rhythmic and harmonic punctuation marks, and though these are dealt out with great parsimony, one must admit that they are always perfectly apt.

Other less important elements in his style are nevertheless worth mentioning, such as his changes of register. Basie displays a certain fondness for extremely high notes (*When the Sun Goes Down*), especially during the final measures of a piece (*Saint Louis Boogie, Swingin' the Blues*); he dips into the bass much less often (*Farewell Blues*). He often uses riffs, but does not like to repeat them; in this respect *Dirty Dozens* is rather exceptional. However, Basie sometimes plays a series of syncopated chords in alternate hands (*I Never Knew*), drawing, of course, a maximum of swing from this device. His choruses seldom contain quotations; the most notable is probably an allusion to *Salt Peanuts* which turns up at the end of *One O'clock Boogie* (perhaps as a tribute to his successor Gillespie).

2

We now come to the most interesting aspect of Basie's art, which has yet to be explored for its deepest meanings. For indeed there is only one domain in which Basie has made an original contribution to jazz, and that is the domain of rhythm. I am not merely referring to the general swing of his playing—we all know that Basie is a past master of swing—but to his rhythmic imagination, the way he builds phrases by organizing note values, attacks, intensities, and pauses.

At first glance Basie does not seem to use a very wide range of note values. Because of his repertory and his allegiance to the blues spirit, he is often inclined to use only triplets and triplet derivatives. Irrational values appear only in very slow tempos (*Blue and Sentimental, Basie's Basement*). Double time is also fairly rare and never protracted (*How Long Blues*[4]). Syncopated notes appear frequently in both hands. However, the rhythmic displacements of the left hand figures in the statement of *Café Society Blues* (1942) prove that Basie had not only mastered the rhythmic problems facing jazzmen of his day but was also aware of those his successors would eventually have to solve. The introduction to *Backstage at Stuff's* contains a syncopated ascending passage whose structure reveals Basie's keen feeling for the swinging potentialities of mixed note values. Basie knows what even a moderately complex rhythm can do. In *Farewell Blues* he uses syncopation to vary the theme, just as Arm-

Fig. 2

strong does; but whereas the Count generally places the syncopated note groups before the non-syncopated ones, Louis places them after (Fig. 2).

---

[4] Columbia version.

As we can see, none of these traits set Count Basie apart from the other fine pianists of his generation. When he plays "in phrases" he often builds up his solos—in part, at least—from apparently disconnected elements, melodic and rhythmic "figures" separated by stretches of silence. This is where we tackle the real "Basie problem," and a fascinating problem it is as it contains the key to the great originality of a pianist whose extraordinary sense of rhythm has struck the imagination of, among others, the composer Michel Fano, one of the outstanding members of the young French school of row composition.

For indeed, silence plays a very important part in Basie's music. He is the first jazzman to have had such a fine intuitive grasp of "musical silence"; besides Basie, only the very great improvisers have had this feeling for silence at all: Armstrong, Parker, Lester Young, etc. Silence is present everywhere in his music, even in the most conventional passages. Thus, in this typical example drawn from *Comin' Out Party*[5] the phrase has scarcely gathered momentum when it

Fig. 3

stops to "breathe" for three whole beats (Fig. 3). One of the main characteristics of Basie's style is that the music is continually allowed to rest while the rhythm section takes over.

[5] Two other noteworthy features in the same phrase are the elision of of the last sixteenth note and, in the next measure, the accentuation of the syncopated chord (variation of intensity).

These pauses sometimes result in a gradual dilution of the melodic line (*Shine On Harvest Moon*).

But this use of silence becomes most interesting when pauses are combined with autonomous notes or figures to form structures of sound and silence. Only then does the complexity of Basie's rhythmic vocabulary become fully apparent. The presence of long note-values, rarely found in a jazz-piano idiom, takes on a deep rhythmic significance. This type of value, composed of a very short note followed by a very long silence, plays an important role in the slow statement of *Basie's Basement*.

Let us now examine what the biologist would call a "section" of a Basie solo, the first four measures of the third chorus in *Red Wagon*. Fragments of this kind, despite their melodic triviality—or perhaps because of it—best reveal the essence of this music for what it is: a cunning play of "melodic silences" in which the beat of the rhythm section comes to the fore and, acting as a kind of gauge, *actualizes* the notion of Time—silences in which one *waits* for the next piano note without knowing exactly when it will come (the symmetry of the first two figures is merely meant to tease the ear, since we *know* that the third will be displaced). Similar conclusions may be drawn from an analysis of *Basie's Blues* or *Bugle Blues* which, as we have seen, are interesting only as rhythm.

". . . Because of their melodic triviality"; with this remark we begin to see the real meaning of Basie's rejection of melodic invention which seemed so surprising before. He may well have deliberately deprived his music of any harmonic and melodic charm in order to concentrate entirely on experiments in rhythm. Such a thing is quite conceivable; examples of similar "choices" are to be found in the history of Western music

3

Let's widen the scope of our investigations and examine an entire chorus, that of *Doggin' Around*. Silence plays a predominant role in the first measures: the melodic line is reduced to a two-note figure—D flat (blue note 3) and F (dominant—in which the second note is repeated; the figure is repeated a bit later (measure 3) after an anacrusis composed of the same melodic elements (Fig. 4). Thus reduced

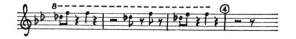

Fig. 4

to a bare minimum, this melodic material bathes, as it were, in silence. Somewhat further on a new note appears—a G; it is sounded five times in alternation with an F, and then the original figure returns in a slightly modified form (Fig. 5).

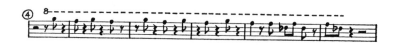

Fig. 5

Need I emphasize the fact that this music carries melodic asceticism to the point where melody almost vanishes completely? Seldom has Basie gone so far in eliminating this dimension from his music. The extreme economy of means enhances the rhythmic element which makes this solo so interesting. The superposition of 3/8 and 4/4 time (measures 4 to 7) is all the more perceptible as the listener's attention is distracted by no melodic or instrumental elements.

The chorus develops on two different levels, rhythmic and melodic. From measures 9 to 16 the time-values grow steadily shorter as their number increases so that by the end of the phrase there are eight to the bar; at the same time Basie widens his note-range and returns to a normal melodic vocabulary. This expansion of the melodic and rhythmic scope culminates in the bridge; here each phrase is a continuous succession of eighth notes while the melodic line is adorned with chromatics and harmonic thirds. The solo ends with a reference to the earlier 3/8 beat (measures 4 to 7), played this time on just one note, G. The last phrase is noteworthy for the brutal rhythmic and melodic contrast with which it begins (Fig. 6).

Fig. 6

As we can see, the chorus's opening figure is presented here in harmonic form. This is an excellent idea, but I feel that the chief interest of this passage lies in the contrast between a very long and a very short note (the ratio is 9 to 1) and especially in the play of intensities between the accented eighth note and the natural decrescendo of the tied whole note. This is far from being an isolated instance in Basie's work; his music is full of rhythmic inventions involving the use of *attack* and *intensity*. I shall cite only three: the first striking measures of his solo in *One O'Clock Boogie;* a brief passage in *The Town Shuffle* in which he sets up contrasts, first between successive figures, then between successive notes; the last chorus in *Shine On Harvest Moon* in which a set of syncopated eighth notes, played pianissimo, is dominated by a long, loud, syncopated note.

Basie's percussive fingers enable him to make the most of these contrasting intensities. The quality of his attack, combined, needless to say, with a perfect sense of the measure, would bring alive far less original rhythmic patterns. This aspect of Basie's techniques is evident in all of his records, but most particularly in *Meet Me at No Special Place, Jive at Five*[6] and *Basie's Basement.*

4

Basie is apparently as reluctant to give other soloists continued support as he is to accompany himself. In other words, his piano performs its role in the rhythm section much the same way as his left hand performs in his solos: soberly, fluidly, and intermittently. At times he may even let the other rhythm players carry on by themselves for several choruses (*Sugar Blues*). He rarely provides a really full-blown accompaniment; in *Every Tub*[7] he uses a stride effect with a syncopated chord at the end of every other measure, one of his favorite devices—but this may be regarded as an exceptional case. Between these two extremes lies a whole range of techniques which he applies, we must admit, with great aptness. In *Harvard Blues* his contribution to the vocal solo and to the full-blown ensemble work in the finale is confined, aside from a few well-placed appoggiatura-acciaccatura, to a syncopated tonic chord slipped in at the end of each tutti phrase as though to summon the next. The punc-

---

[6] Blue Star version.

[7] Blue Star version

tuative role he assigns to the piano is highly suited to that instrument; this is especially noticeable in his *Saint Louis Blues*. I should point out, however, that he is also quite capable of spinning a lively countermelody in "saxophone" style, as in *Good Morning Blues,* one of the few Basie records on which the piano part has any real melodic charm.

Most of the time Basie resembles modern pianists in his use of only brief chords, either on the beat or syncopated. This method does not give the rhythmic substructure as much weight as, say, Clyde Hart's 4/4 playing in *When Lights Are Low,* but what the rhythm section loses in impact it gains in vivacity and variety. Basie may be considered as a precursor in this respect, for though it seems that Earl Hines used this accompanying technique before him, the Count was the first to exploit it thoroughly. Witness the

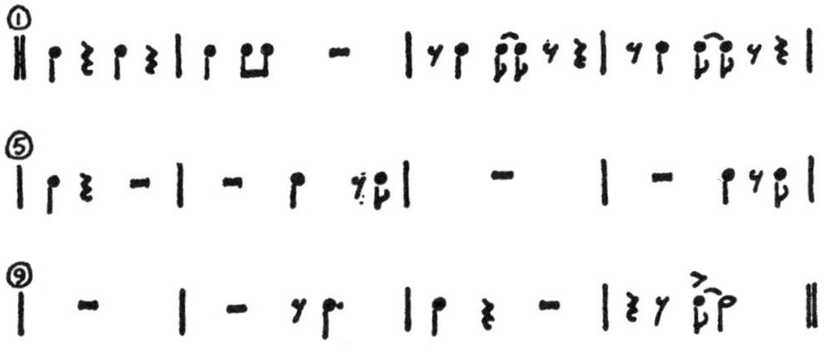

Fig. 7

skillful dosing of symmetry and asymmetry in the rhythmic figures scattered throughout his chorus in *Swingin' the Blues*[8] (Fig. 7).

Basie's sense of rhythm works wonders in a give-and-take

---

[8] Victor version.

with the band or whenever an arrangement calls for his entrance at a given moment. In *Bugle Blues* and *Comin' Out Party,* the single notes which he slips in between the full band figures have a function similar to that of those solo "figures" whose importance in his work I have already pointed out. The dialogue between piano and tutti in *Why Not* and the 3/8 answers to the band riffs in *Saint Louis Boogie* reveal Basie's complete mastery of orchestral problems. Of course there was no reason to expect any less of one of the greatest bandleaders in the history of jazz.

But I can only mention this other side of his talent here. My chief concern has been to show what the Count's original contribution to jazz has been, and to define the essence of his music. If the reader still fails to see in what this consists, if the "Basie riddle" remains intact for him, the fault can only lie with my demonstration.

CHAPTER 11

Basie's Way

It took Count Basie's orchestra more than twenty years to find its style. This is not so long considering that many others, some among the very best, never found theirs at all. [17]

If we compare Basie's best prewar records with his best recent ones, we immediately realize that the center of interest has shifted. Lester Young, Buck Clayton, Dicky Wells, Harry Edison, and Herschel Evans used to monopolize our attention; today it is the band as a whole. Pieces like *Doggin' Around* and *Swingin' the Blues* consisted of one dazzling solo after another which the orchestra seemed merely to usher in and out rather than trying to justify them in any way. Now these solos have given way to a more strictly orchestral conception, of which the best example to date is Frank Foster's fine arrangement of *Shiny Stockings*. Here the solos are embedded into the work like so many gems; they seem to be by-products of the arrangement rather than its reason for being even though they are not nearly so well integrated as the best improvisations of Cootie, Hodges, and Bigard in their Ellington days.

As a matter of fact, the quality of the solos is such that it would no longer justify an exhaustive study of Basie's orchestra. This very fact, however, raises a point which until now has remained obscure; how do these twelve men (I am deliberately disregarding the rhythm section), nine of whom do not display any particular gift for swing in their solos, manage to form the most extraordinary, and assuredly the most "swinging" wind section in the history of jazz? How does a saxophonist or a trombonist, who, in his solos, is clearly incapable of conveying that rhythmic thrill which the great jazzmen produce so easily (and which men as unimaginative as Hampton or Jacquet can also convey) manage, with the help of other equally undistinguished soloists, to produce such extraordinary orchestral swing only five minutes later?

Basie and his arrangers seem to have realized the necessity of a dual form, if not of a dual style. Their approach is based on a perennial contrast between two musical worlds. Phrases designed for full orchestra have always been tailored differently from phrases written for soloists. Arrangers have done their best to accentuate this difference, going so far as to harmonize this or that famous solo (though in practice this was limited to identical instruments and therefore had no effect on tutti scoring). Count Basie's present orchestra owes its originality to exactly the opposite approach, as is apparent in the best arrangements—I may even say the only good arrangements—in its repertory. *Shiny Stockings*, despite a rather labored beginning due to the mediocrity of the tune itself, carries this static quality to a maximum in the finale, the seven brass and five saxophones being handled as a single section.

Two factors further strengthen the impression of motionlessness—I almost wrote immobility—created by this piece: the tempo and the density of the written texture. The tempo is very hard to define; it is somewhere between slow and medium slow. Its metronomic value ($\bf{J} = 136$) allows for a perfectly balanced dosage of the triplets and triplet figures (syncopated or not) which Basie has never abandoned (their rehabilitation in modern jazz is due largely to his influence). The resultant static quality is further accentuated by the use of a two-beat. Given these premises, each phrase is bound to be extremely loose and airy in its horizontal movement and vertically very compact. Conversely the soloist will naturally strive to free his own phrasing from this constraint, in the hope that the greater mobility obtained by switching into double time will afford him the breathing space that the work's substructure will not. The result is an absolute contrast.

Supposing, however, we were to imagine some sort of correspondence or exchange between these two elements. Would the sharp outlines of the ensemble phrasing assigned by Frank Foster to an entire wind section still make sense as jazz if played by a soloist? Certainly not. These phrases are meaningful only when endowed with their *specific weight* and can acquire this weight only when played simultaneously on at least ten horns. Phrases of this sort would sound much too "light" on just three brasses and three saxes. Thus, we are dealing here with what we may call "massive phrasing."

All of this constitutes such an obvious aesthetic truth that it makes one wonder whether there is any grounds at all for the orchestral notions of the arrangers who supply Kenton (Billy Holman) and Ellington (Billy Strayhorn), especially as these notions are still in the experimental stage and have never, to my knowledge, been crowned with a complete technical and aesthetic success. Contrapuntal writing for the big band may be regarded as an error, particularly in so far as it tends to reduce the specific weight of the wind section and dilute rather than condense the phrase; it is now as much a thing of the past as the old habit of scoring by sections. This type of counterpoint is probably valid only in middle-sized ensembles (six to ten horns); big bands would seem to be suited only to massive phrasing, though an orchestra involving several different "levels" might provide a composite solution by combining a very large wind section with various groups of soloists. This would be a more elaborate form of the solution proposed by seventeenth-century Italian composers in their concerti grossi, and timidly revived by Duke Ellington in *Jam a Ditty*.

This notion of massive phrasing provides the answer to the questions raised a moment ago. Most of the musicians in Basie's orchestra, probably for lack of rhythmic imagination, swing only moderately well in their solos; long rehearsals have taught them to play to perfection a completely different type of phrase and to convey, almost mechanically, the massive swing implicit in it. We have all been struck by the well-oiled mechanism of Count Basie's "jazz factory"— the expression is not new, but do we realize what it means in terms of the individual musician?—which manages, nearly every evening, to "swing it" with the selfsame remarkable intensity. There is obviously very little room in these musicians' lives for the joy of fresh discovery. Their program is practically always the same. Their job is to put the same accent on the same note in the same passage of the same score night after night, and in this respect these super-robots must have the patience and passivity of the musicians in a symphony orchestra. (Though actually theirs is much greater, for who ever heard of a symphony orchestra with such a limited repertory?)

Hence we see that there is a place in jazz for mere executors who are also jazzmen, despite the widespread belief that a jazz musician is always, to some extent, creative.

No one can deny that they are jazzmen, since they swing. But the fact that they *create* nothing, not even the swing that they produce so efficiently, will probably be a bone of contention for some time to come. Wrongly so, I feel, for creativeness, after all, means a fresh approach, trial and error, a leap into the void. Count Basie's men know nothing of the sort; they live in a kind of frozen, immutable perfection, which they have helped to create only to the extent that a bricklayer "creates" a building. They themselves did not conceive it; someone else—the arranger—did so for them, and Basie's (or Marshall Royal's) role of mentor is at least as important as theirs. Moreover, most of the work is done in rehearsal and the finishing touches applied in the first few concerts.

From then on the musicians are as passive as their symphonic counterparts. There is no basic difference between the work of a saxophone player in Basie's orchestra and that of a French horn player in the Orchestre de la Suisse Romande; the horn player re-creates Debussy's music under the guidance of Ansermet, who has "digested" the work for him, while the saxophonist actualizes the music of Frank Foster or Ernie Wilkins according to directions given him by Basie and his arrangers.

And we may be sure that these directions are very precise, not to say rigid; our performer is allowed no initiative whatsoever. He has learned to produce swing through the intermediary of the thought and sensibility of other men, and these ultimately clothe him in such a hard, thick shell that the individual vanishes completely. He becomes a cog in the wheel, dedicated to playing the same piece—and therefore producing the same effects—night after night; and every night he has to fool the audience, just as an actor fools it with his thousandth performance in a given role. Needless to say, there is absolutely nothing spontaneous about his playing; for him, swing is a job, and the job comes first. This paradox is typical of jazz.

Of course, I do not mean to belittle in any way the merits of these instrumentalists; their work is of a very high quality by the standards of both music and jazz. Though only passive performers, as such they are in a class by themselves. The extraordinary precision of the final band passages in *Shiny Stockings* is unquestionably the work of these master craftsmen. But the even more extraordinary conception behind these passages, so astonishingly modern in their restraint, was devised by Frank Foster (and perhaps by Basie or Royal as well). This is where Basie's band snaps the bonds of neoclassicism and steps boldly forth into the world of modern jazz. Indeed, the gradual accumulation of violence which characterizes this piece came straight out of the cool jazz of the early fifties; it is this principle which prevents the first wind trills from being blown full force (as they would have been in the days of "hot expressionism"), allowing for the splendid, final release of all that pent-up energy (and gradual though this release may be, it is nonetheless real).

While Frank Foster is truly creative so long as he has a pencil in his hand, his spirit of invention seems to desert him completely in his concert solos with the band (or even in a set at Birdland). With the exception of Joe Newman and Thad Jones, the soloists have all been contaminated by the orchestra's workaday attitude. Not only do they make very little effort to achieve variety, but, worse still, they are so afraid of risks that they've lost all ambition. The banality of some of the solos they play over and over again, almost note for note, is unworthy of such a fine orchestra. Inversely, Joe Williams has achieved a kind of routine perfection. Nothing resembles one of his renditions of *Every Day* so much as the one he gave the night before, unless it be the one he is going to give the night after; touches which seem completely "spontaneous," such as the "hoarse" vocal effect in *Every Day*, are astonishingly alike from one performance to the next. Williams is a perfect Basie product; his singing seems to have no aim other than to imitate his records. Let's close our eyes for a second: is that Joe Williams. . . or one of his records? And yet at times one does enjoy hearing him, for he is very talented.

To all appearances, Basie's orchestra has great difficulty finding fresh material. Stylistic perfection is a hard thing to maintain, especially when it depends upon a whole set of circumstances and when the music is not the work of a single mind. Yet this perfection is essential. The arrangements that the orchestra has included in its repertory lately are not all of the same caliber. Some are downright bad, like that version of *April in Paris* which is said to be Basie's biggest commercial success since *Every Day* but which, musically speaking, is indefensible; the arrangement doesn't suit the theme and the theme doesn't suit the orchestra. Those of us who appreciate Basie's sober, pleasant, dignified attitude on the podium hate to see him stoop to "grandstanding" when he plays this ballad, repeating the last few measures as an encore. This procedure, of which Louis Armstrong is so fond, must be wholeheartedly condemned, no matter what the value of the piece itself. Let us hope that the Count will give up this cheap applause-gathering device— it is not essential to the survival of his band—and make up his program with greater rigor than he displayed on his last trip to Paris in October, 1956. Even at the risk of outward monotony, Count Basie's orchestra ought to play nothing but blues or arrangements steeped in the spirit of the blues. Recently Francy Boland has done some writing for Basie; much can be expected of this very gifted arranger for whom the blues is still very much alive. It might also be well for Basie to do away with fast tempos; the orchestra seems to have difficulty maintaining them, and in any case it swings best in the medium-slow pieces like *Shiny Stockings* and *Every Day*. The real problem facing Count Basie's band is not how to enlarge its range but rather how to achieve maximum diversity without quitting the field where it is second to none.

It would be a mistake to expect Count Basie's orchestra to develop into the great modern band we are all waiting for, and which neither Stan Kenton nor Dizzy Gillespie has yet succeeded in creating. The Count and his men are giving us a wonderful lesson in classicism; better still, they have managed not only to last as an orchestra but to develop as well, and even, on a strictly technical level, to improve. This is what makes them unique. A fresh approach to the big jazz orchestra will stem from some other source, and I expect that the Ellington spirit, which has lain dormant for fifteen years now, will play a major part in it.

CHAPTER 12

Benny Carter as I See Him

The title of this chapter may cause some surprise, and requires a preliminary explanation.[18] I have scruples about writing an essay on Benny Carter, for he is one of the few jazzmen about whom I disagree with most of the good musicians of my generation. A few years ago I expressed value judgments concerning Jimmy Noone, Kid Ory, Johnny Dodds, Roy Eldridge, and Teddy Wilson which went against the grain of general opinion—I mean *public* opinion. But at least I did not have the feeling that I was the only one who thought the way I did; a good many musicians would gladly have seconded those judgments. Will the same be true in this case? Nothing could be less sure. I have never heard anything but praise in connection with Benny Carter. During the German Occupation, memories of his trip to France were still vivid in the minds of Paris jazzmen and they were unanimous in their praise. More recently, a great musician of the next generation paid Carter the tribute of ranking him among the principal precursors of modern jazz.[1] I have to confess that I have never shared this all but unanimous enthusiasm. In fact my reservations have become

---

[1] Kenny Clarke, "Voyons les Choses en Face" in *Jazz Hot,* June, 1950.

increasingly stronger; ten years ago I would have agreed to rank Benny Carter among the fifteen or twenty most important soloists in the history of jazz; today I would not.

I hope the reader will excuse the personal tone of this long introduction; it is designed to put him on his guard. For once I intend to depart from the rule of objectivity which is, I feel, indispensable for any constructive criticism. This chapter expresses a purely subjective point of view, a strictly personal insight.

1

Between 1920 and 1930 jazzmen were primarily concerned with enlarging their range of expression; they wanted to add a few more colors to a palette that had been previously limited to the wail of the blues and the frenzy of the "hot" style. At the same time, financial imperatives made them adopt the highly sentimental repertory of Tin Pan Alley, but the Negro's sensibility, largely predominant in the good jazz of the period, was ill-prepared to cope with that kind of material. The result was a wave of sentimentalism which left its indelible mark on a great many records. A certain type of badly controlled vibrato, already dubious in the blues, became even uglier when applied to lighter tunes, and certain kinds of inflection began to spread like cankers.

In this respect, the following observation, made by Lucien Malson in connection with King Oliver's *Someday Sweetheart,* is none too severe: "*Someday Sweetheart* borders on the ridiculous; unfortunately it contains no evidently humorous intentions. One can only suppose that this is the way King Oliver's Syncopators thought the white man's slow, sentimental fox trot ought to be played. The statement of the theme on the tuba (!) is grotesque to say the least, but words cannot describe the exquisite bad taste of the solo that follows; to think that it is the work of Barney Bigard, regarded as the best Negro tenor player of his day! One can hardly believe it!"[2]

At first glance this reference to Barney Bigard may seem surprising; after all, a few years later, he was doing perfectly valid work with Ellington and his men. And yet this case was not unique. When the Negro tried to refurbish the white man's ballad he often went astray. Joe Smith, Buster Bailey, Otto Hardwicke and countless others were contaminated by a lamentable aesthetic conception of which Jimmy Noone's *After You've Gone* may be regarded as the most perfect expression.

And yet just before 1930 a few musicians began to react. Taking their cue from Louis Armstrong, young jazzmen adopted a more rigorous—or more ironic—attitude toward the ballad; among them were Coleman Hawkins, Fats Waller, Johnny Hodges, and Benny Carter. There was less sentimental effusion, and if tears were still shed, they were discreet and no longer had the same sickening effect. At first, of course, this change was felt only in a small minority of musicians; around 1932 a great many saxophone sections still used that whining vibrato and doleful inflection that were the rule a few years earlier.

I have mentioned Benny Carter as one of the pioneers of this liberating movement. I wish to make it very clear that Carter can in no way be associated with the musicians of the previous period. Better than any other musician, perhaps, he represents an era of jazz, which, for want of a better term, we may call "preclassical," and which extends from around 1927 to 1935. While preparing for the perfectly balanced jazz of the period 1935–1945, Benny Carter and his genera-

---

[2] Lucien Malson, *Les Maîtres du Jazz*, Presses Universitaires de France, 1952.

tion were also destroying the past. But, as is almost always the case, his music remained linked to ideas he was trying to destroy. Carter was born in 1906 and grew up in the atmosphere of the twenties. Strong though his subsequent reaction to it was, that period could not fail to leave its mark on him. We must not be surprised, therefore, to find that his work contains, between two layers of hard, glittering metal, a stratum of softer ore, an undefinable hint of sentimentality which he would have avoided had he been born ten years later.

2

The chief problem with Benny Carter is, I feel, the problem of the instrument he plays best, the alto sax; in other words the problem of that instrument's timbre, its tone. This is a problem which is not confined to jazz circles. Classical saxophonists are perfectly familiar with it, as well. In France the overwhelming influence of the accomplished virtuoso Marcel Mule has led them to adopt a cello-like tone which is pleasing to the ear and which has come to be identified with the instrument itself. This powerful, sonorous tone, with its rich, even vibrato, still has strong supporters in the world of jazz. The alto saxophone, they say, is designed to "sing melodious phrases"; for them Benny Carter represents a kind of perfection, and they are right: to my knowledge no jazz saxophonist has greater control over his tone in every register of the instrument. His high notes, in particular, are exceptionally full and true. Saxophone players from the Conservatoire—in other words the disciples of Marcel Mule—all make fun of Charlie Parker but admire Benny Carter unreservedly. This, I feel, is very significant.

Why is it that, as a composer, I have never, until very

recently, been able to write a saxophone part in even the most insignificant film score? Whenever I have tried to devise one, a kind of conditioned reflex would make me hear, in my "inner ear," the tone of Mule's saxophone. Now that tone, if I may be forgiven the expression, is an effeminate tone. Though it has every imaginable charm, it lacks that essential factor, virility. Too intent upon being pretty, it can never attain real beauty.

I have the same aversion to Benny Carter's tone (to keep this criticism on a strictly personal level, I might say the same allergy). True, we are dealing with jazz, but this is not an extenuating circumstance, quite the contrary. As a matter of fact I may be exaggerating the subjective side of my reactions; today's sensibility, conditioned as it is by nearly ten years of modern jazz, may simply no longer tolerate a certain form of anachronistic sentimentality, even when it has been filtered through a musical sensibility as lucid as Carter's!

Though effeminate, his tone is nonetheless rich. Carter has that taste for lavish sound which characterizes the Hawkins school. This may be the source of his error, for a tone which sounds rich and full on the tenor sax—a virile instrument if ever there was one—will sound overly rich and even flaccid on the alto. When we hear Hawkins play, even in a slow tempo, we have no doubt but what we are listening to a master of "hot expressionism." Benny Carter's style, on the other hand, often seems to lack tension. His rich but rather lifeless vibrato and his very full tone all make for an elegant style, but not a firm one.

He seldom plays blues, but when he does he has to exaggerate his effects in order to stay in the right mood; the growl in *Apologies* (with Mezzrow) and the syncopated repetition and sustained high notes in *Bay Back Boogie* are rather unusual in his work.

Can Benny Carter be regarded, then, as a precursor of the relaxed style that typifies the "cool" jazz of today? Though raised in a tradition of "hot" music, it did not suit his natural temperament, and his considerable influence during the thirties was certainly responsible, to some extent, for recent developments. His music, however, was not actually a part of this evolution; it merely helps to explain it. In many ways his style is diametrically opposed to that of "cool" jazzmen; his tone is too resonant, too ornate, his manner too elaborate. The resulting contradictions in his music could not be fully apparent ten years ago but our experience with modern jazz makes them stand out vividly today.

It is generally agreed that, from a purely musical standpoint, Benny Carter is one of the most gifted of all jazzmen. Critics and musicians alike pay tribute to his keen ear and his capacity for invention. Carter certainly deserves this praise, but it seems to me that in his records, at least, he has seldom given complete satisfaction. His qualities as a musician are self-evident and yet I feel that his defects are just as obvious. Carter has a taste for facileness which leads him, all too often, to play the first thing that comes under his fingers; he has this weakness in common with hundreds of other soloists, but it is emphasized by the high quality of his improvisation.

Even his phrasing is open to criticism. Here his choice of techniques is not always felicitous. Elegance, of course, is his primary concern, and at his best he attains a level of purity worthy of the greatest jazz improvisers (*A Tisket A Tasket* with Teddy Wilson; *When Lights Are Low* and *Hot Mallets* with Lionel Hampton). Sometimes however, this elegance is a bit affected; the tongued high notes in *More Than You Know* (with Teddy Wilson) may have seemed "pretty" in 1939, but it is the kind of effect that goes out of date quickly. This abuse of tonguing recurs frequently in his work (I shall cite only *Scandal in A Flat*). *Savoy Stampede* (1939) brings to light a number of other weaknesses in Benny Carter's phrasing, such as his use of sustained, rather slack vibrato alternating with semi-staccato notes. I am aware that this alternation was Carter's way of making up for the impression of general monotony produced by his overly even phrasing. It seems to me that he would have done better to use a real system of accents, as Hodges, and later Parker, did. This lack—or near lack—of accents, which makes it hard to listen to Benny Carter for any length of time, is by no means offset by the use of other techniques which are simply incompatible with one another.[3]

From a rhythmic standpoint, Benny Carter's is not a syncopated style. For him syncopation is merely a further element of contrast and in his phrasing he makes good use of it to break the monotony of long periods (played in a single breath). *Smack* (with Hawkins) is full of syncopated notes, and *On the Bumpy Road to Love* (with Teddy Wilson) contains whole strings of them; these are extreme cases, however. One has to admit that in the rhythmic layout of his phrasing, Carter displays undeniable musicianship. The eight measure chorus in *Some of These Days* (1945) may be cited for its exemplary rhythmic freedom. The displaced rhythms in *Smack* are more contrived, perhaps, as is the accelerated delivery obtained in *On the Bumpy Road to Love* and *My Buddy* by replacing ternary values (triplets) with binary ones (eighth notes); this device, at least, is of his

---

[3] It should be pointed out, however, that Carter's use of inflection displays perfect sobriety.

own invention. Carter seldom uses double time and when he does adopt it (*Scandal in A Flat*) he does not make the most of it from the standpoint of swing.

3

Carter's melodic inventions, like his phrasing, are sinuous, graceful, and elegant. As we have already seen, these three qualities favor a certain insipidness, which finds its melodic expression in Carter's affection for broken chords (*Savoy Stampede*), melodic lines composed of ascending thirds (*Sugar* with Teddy Wilson and, above all, the famous chorus in *Crazy Rhythm*) and, more generally, in certain facile tricks which just seem to "slip out." Moreover, those "period clichés" which crop up in Hawkins's phrasing, sometimes creep into Carter's as well (the same one comes up twice in one of his best solos, *On the Bumpy Road to Love*). These are the only drawbacks to Carter's improvisational gifts, which, in other respects, are well above average, thanks to his exceptionally keen ear. Despite his brilliant technique he occasionally seems hindered by a tempo which is too fast for him (*Riff Romp*); on the other hand, he is never troubled by even the most unusual chord sequence.

Carter's melodic phrasing can take alternative forms: it may wind about freely, or else be centered around certain notes. His "winding" solos consist in a series of ascending waves which are constantly interrupted as the phrase suddenly plunges back into the bass, only to rise again a few measures, or even a few beats, later. Carter is very fond of this type of contour, the sharper edges of which are rounded off by his full tone (*My Buddy; Sunday*). He also likes brief flights in the highest register (*On the Bumpy Road to Love*). The "polarized"solos, on the other hand, assign a privileged role to one or two notes—tonic and/or dominant—around which the rest of the melodic fabric converges fairly systematically (*A Tisket A Tasket* with Teddy Wilson; *Sendin' the Vipers* with Mezz Mezzrow).

We must also give Carter credit for his great skill at chorus building, as displayed in his double chorus on the blues theme *Bay Back Boogie*. Both sections of this solo begin with a blue note; it is syncopated the first time, and held in a high register the second. In both cases the tension created is gradually worked off by an increasingly flexible phrasing. The over-all balance of this solo is, of course, quite exceptional. The end of the chorus in *Crazy Rhythm*, for example, seems rather tame and is not, in any case, on a level with the flights of lyricism with which it began. Carter's sense of construction is generally more apparent in the details of his playing. From this standpoint his solo in *Smack* is full of interesting inventions: the clever bass punctuation at the beginning, the symmetrical motives in the bridge (an idea which Hawkins picks up later in the same piece and makes even more brilliant use of), and the melodic development of a riff at the beginning of the second chorus. And of course we mustn't forget the delicate precision of those eight-measure gems which he slips into *Some of These Days* and, above all, into Hampton's *Hot Mallets* and *When Lights Are Low*.

Though one may say that Carter cannot "go the distance," no one can question his absolute mastery as a miniaturist. This is where his supreme elegance finds its reward. I should gladly give every record he ever made for just these three little solos and all the music they contain. Each ends with a melodic invention which is sheer perfection in its simplicity, a "peroration" that is all the more apt as it actually constitutes a very subtle transition into the music that follows.

There is much more to be said about this musician who has recorded a great deal and whose influence was tremendous (even Parker shows signs of it in *Groovin' High*). I feel that Johnny Hodges, among his contemporaries, and Charlie Parker and Lee Konitz among his successors, had more valid approaches to the alto sax, but this may simply be because these musicians come closer to my own temperament. In absolute value Benny Carter may well be Hodges's equal—though not Parker's of course—but he undoubtedly has certain failings; a flair for accents and their correct placing would have enabled him to produce a swing worthy of his musicianship. Such as he is, Benny Carter often disappoints me; sometimes he even bores me. If it comes to a showdown, I have to admit that I don't think his music as a whole will stand the test of time. On the other hand, I cannot believe that we will soon forget an artist who on some occasions, however brief, has so thoroughly delighted us. Great things can be achieved on a small scale.

CHAPTER 13

The "Genius" of Art Tatum

What is genius? [19]

Is it enough that a man's creative powers, the fertility of his imagination, his good taste, sensibility, and technique be unsurpassed by any other jazz musician for the lucky man in question to be regarded *ipso facto* as a genius? In his introduction to the set of Art Tatum records, Norman Granz does not seem to shrink from this assertion. He ventures even farther when he entitles this set "The Genius of Art Tatum" (not without having observed at the outset that in the past much abuse has been made of the word "genius").

Mr. Granz is certainly not afraid of a risk, though in this case the risk is limited by the very nature of the subject at hand, since there is probably no other jazz musician who is so unanimously admired by his fellows. It is very hard to find any jazz pianists, even among the most modern, who do not regard Tatum as the greatest of them all. This extraordinary skillful performer quite literally fascinates younger pianists. And how can they help admiring a man who conceives and executes ideas which they themselves, in so far as they conceive them, are incapable of executing?

Let us therefore concede that Tatum is the greatest of all

jazz pianists, that the sum of his creative powers, imagination, good taste, sensibility, and technique is greater than that of any other jazz musician. I do not believe that this is true but for the sake of argument let us say that it is. Should we, however, ascribe an absolute value to an "average score," no matter how amazingly high, when dealing with a field in which certain factors (some of which Mr. Granz omits altogether) are infinitely more important than others? Certainly not. Genius is not the result of any average; nor can it be evaluated in terms of one.

The release of these five long playing records entirely devoted to Tatum constitute an event the importance of which should be obvious to everyone in jazz. Tatum had previously recorded a great deal, of course, but this phenomenal musician had never before been given such a completely free hand; his style had always been cramped in one way or another—by the stop watch (in the days of 78 rpm), by the presence of a live audience or, when playing with a group, by the style of his partners. Here Tatum was free at last, and for this pianist, probably less at home in an orchestra than any of the great jazz pianists, the fact of being alone at the keyboard, at liberty to improvise for ten minutes on a single theme if he felt like it, should probably be a decisive factor in his favor. The truth is that few jazz musicians have ever been provided with such an opportunity to exhibit the full range of their talents. As Mr. Granz puts it, Tatum was being recorded for posterity.

Mr. Granz has done his duty as a producer; my duty as a critic is to conduct an impartial examination of the result. The fact that the recording is technically remarkable, endowing the piano with great "presence," further contributes to making this an exceptional set of records. It is now possible for the European critic, usually at a disadvantage when he has not been able personally to hear the musician under examination, to have a fairly accurate notion of what the American listener must feel as he gets to know Tatum in the night club or concert hall. This set should be looked upon as a survey of Tatum's work, conducted by the famous pianist himself at the peak of his career.

Has the freedom referred to above been extended to Tatum's repertory? Did his choice of tunes stem from purely musical considerations? It seems indeed that no pressure was brought to bear on the pianist and that pieces like *Body and Soul, Humoresque, The Man I Love,* and *Begin the Beguine* are really "Tatum's favorites." Here, I feel, is where I must begin to be critical; for this choice is a little too facile. The table of contents of these records might have been conceived as a sort of anthology of the most beautiful jazz tunes, with pieces like *Black and Blue, Jordu, Lover Man* and *Squeeze Me.*[20] As it stands the collection deliberately sacrifices the beautiful melody to the sentimental ditty, the authentic jazz tune to the hit-song. It even makes room, as we shall see, for the most dubious form of semi-classical piece.

In itself, however, the choice of themes should not determine the success or failure of a jazz record. This depends upon the musician's reaction to the material selected. Louis Armstrong has managed to confer real dignity on silly little tunes merely by shifting a few accents and altering a few note-values; Fats Waller could endow the most stupidly sentimental songs with an unaffected, witty, and poetic character; Charlie Parker would use his sleight of hand to juggle with bits and pieces of a tune he was supposed to be developing but which he would keep diabolically hidden in the folds of his magic cape; Lester Young, in the very first measures of a melodic exposition, would sometimes switch to a completely new tune that was like a negative image of the original, a cleaned up, retouched, and disturbing image.

All these approaches are valid, but what is Tatum's method? Unfortunately he has chosen the most conventional. Any jazz pianist, even the most obscure cocktail pianist, ornaments a tune as he plays it; in other words, he contrives to vary the theme, either by adding "personal" harmonies or by interspersing the main motives with arabesques, arpeggios, or other virtuoso figures designed to contrast with the simpler melodic lines around them; and, of course, this also gives him a chance to show off his virtuosity. It is this purely decorative conception that Tatum has adopted. He makes no attempt to transcend the theme; he is content with the usual game, though, needless to say, he plays it better than anyone else. His technique and imagination, superior to those of other pianists, enable him to win hands down in a contest one wishes he had avoided altogether.

In actual practice this lack of ambition appears in a series of thematic statements played "out of tempo" which take up far too much space on these records for my taste. What is the point of these statements? One could understand a limited pianist's wanting to avoid monotony at all costs; with such a modest goal in view the "out of tempo" exposition is fairly justified; in fact it would be surprising if certain pianists didn't resort to it. But Tatum is no ordinary pianist.

The method does add a certain element of variety, but this advantage is slight in comparison with the major disadvantage that accompanies it; for when the tempo is abandoned, if only for a few bars, so is the swing. And once the spell of swing is broken, it is hard not to judge the music on its merits alone, in terms of its pure musical density. It then takes a lot of indulgence to ascribe any superior qualities to that formless torrent in which new ideas pop up only infrequently. Tatum does, of course, display great virtuosity and an uncommon flair for harmony; now and then he even tries to bring an element of surprise into his endlessly meandering statements. But his vast imagination strives in vain to enliven themes so intrinsically feeble that only a drastic reappraisal could possibly save them, the very reappraisal which Tatum did not have the courage to undertake.

As I have already said, these statements' chief defect is their exaggerated length. One of them—in *There'll Never Be Another You*—lasts nearly three minutes and is followed by a coda (also "out of tempo") which is almost as long! Fortunately, when Tatum shifts back into a jazz tempo his music changes character and often displays the very best side of his talent. Sometimes these transitions are almost imperceptible; the tempo slips into a musical context from which it was entirely absent, gradually asserting a firmer beat with each new measure (cf. *Louise*). At others the transition is abrupt; the tempo returns suddenly, producing an effect of contrast which has a "wrenching" effect on the listener (cf. *Humoresque*). I should also point out the "false starts" in fast tempo in *The Man I Love*. All of these things are excellent.

The finest moments of this set are found in the improvised passages. Tatum does his best by a theme when he seems to forget about it completely. His capacity for renewing melodic material increases proportionally as he frees himself from the material in question. There are too many interesting inventions on these ten record sides for me to cite all of them. In any case, I have no intention of analysing Tatum's style here. Let me simply point out that while a number of the virtuoso runs he uses soon prove to be mere recipes—I especially have in mind a sort of "improved arpeggio" which he employs a great deal—others on the contrary, are authentic musical inventions. Tatum likes to take advantage of breaks in the beat to slip in one of his long rumbling spirals; he borrowed this trick from Earl Hines, but his incomparable technical superiority enables him to turn it to more consistent advantage. Though elsewhere he is still faithful to the Waller stride or to tenths in the bass à la Teddy Wilson, Tatum often suspends the 4/4 beat in this way without changing the tempo. The resulting "suggested beat" may disturb certain listeners, while the gaps which remain unfilled by any drums or double bass may puzzle those who think that a distinct afterbeat is the whole secret of swing. In my opinion, it is precisely the suggestive quality of these unexpressed beats which constitutes the most absorbing aspect of Art Tatum's style.

These breaks in the beat give a free rein to the left hand, and Tatum often takes this opportunity to work out subtle rhythmic combinations with the right. This is when he best succeeds in creating the impression of an orchestral style rich in potentialities; this is also when he comes closest to modern jazz. The best side of Tatum's musical personality is reflected, not so much in his technique—it is a bit too uniformly brilliant—, nor in his harmony—his use of altered and superposed chords becomes a bit too monotonous—, but in the rhythmic ingenuity that he displays in just this kind of passage.

Tatum's harmonic adornments, rhythmic combinations and serpentine runs form a purely decorative mosaic. And it would seem that the notions of decoration and ornamentation, which automatically come to mind in examining this set of records, are Tatum's primary concern (notably in *This Can't Be Love, Memories of You* and *Begin the Be-*

guine). In the long run, an overabundance of decorative effects cannot fail to detract from the continuity and even the unity of musical discourse, and Tatum, I feel, is too subtle a musician to be unaware of this. Has Tatum deliberately chosen to place this limitation on his art, or has this great pianist, out of complacency, simply shied away from goals which are, admittedly, difficult to reach? There is no ready answer to this question, but the fact that it can be raised at all should cast a doubt on the durability of Tatum's work. Complacency is not the key to immortality.

A few words remain to be said about the semiclassical pieces which Tatum has seen fit to keep in his repertory, pieces which have very little to do with jazz. Here it is no longer possible to believe in that "good taste" vaunted by Mr. Granz in his introduction. True, Tatum does some nice things with his jazzed up variations on Dvořák's *Humoresque,* though he needn't have handled it so roughly in the statement of the theme; it is very hard, on the other hand, to find any excuse for his *Elegy.* Our entire musical education, our whole cultural background, based as it is upon the prime necessity of masterpieces, rebels at such a thing. Moreover, I can think of nothing quite so ridiculous in the entire European semiclassical repertory as Massenet's *Elegy.* And it's no use claiming that Tatum transfigures everything he touches, for here is a specific case in which nothing is transfigured in the least. This little arrangement resembles, both in form and content the encore pieces that a pianist like Horowitz will sometimes defiantly fling to the snobs, musically empty display pieces for virtuoso fingers. Tatum, so timid in other respects, throws caution to the winds when he lays himself open to such a comparison; since this piece contains absolutely no music in any but the lowest sense of the word, and precious little jazz, we can only judge the virtuoso. In this light, and compared with the perfection of a Horowitz, how can one fail to hear the inaccuracies, the uneven fingerings, and a whole range of minute imperfections which deprive these exercises of their last possible justification?

One cannot be too severe with errors of this sort. But it would be unfair to magnify them, since these execrable interludes are actually quite unimportant by comparison with a piece as fine as *Tenderly*. They merely serve to complete the candid self-portrait that Tatum has given us on these five records, and to strengthen our impression of extreme unevenness. To be sure, unevenness is not always irreconcilable with genius, but when the work of a genius is uneven it is generally through an excess of daring, rarely through excessive complacency. The many impurities that can be detected in Tatum's style all stem from the same source. With a bit more rigor and a bit more daring Tatum might have developed his brilliant gifts along completely different lines. If, in the last analysis, and having paid tribute to his great merits, I refuse to regard Tatum as a musician of genius, this is because it seems obvious to me that his very conception of jazz will prevent his ever attaining a level of true artistic creation. In conclusion I should like to quote this splendid phrase of Michel de Ghelderode: "The secret of genius is cruelty." It is this cruelty that is altogether lacking in Tatum.

CHAPTER 14

Bags' Microgroove

The Recorded Works of Milt Jackson

1

Some ten years ago, just after the war, the firmament of jazz was lit by the uncanny light of a few new, ascending stars.[21] In the wake of Parker, Gillespie, and Monk a whole galaxy of soloists, all under twenty-three, set out to prove that modern jazz was not the monopoly of a few, but a powerful movement that was to sweep away all the habits left over from the swing era. These young men displayed such dazzling gifts that from the very outset they seemed on a par with the best. In the first flush of enthusiasm, Max Roach, Bud Powell, Fats Navarro, Al Haig, Miles Davis, Sonny Stitt, and Milt Jackson were all hailed as the equals of their greatest predecessors. Some of them already deserved their reputations; others still had a long way to go. These, we now realize, had not shown any substantial proof of their talent, but merely brilliant promises, no matter how famous they may already have been.

In at least one instance these promises were fulfilled. Milt Jackson's career, now in its tenth year, has followed an ascending curve the like of which is hard to find in the history of jazz. Once again we in France must appraise a jazzman on the basis of his recordings alone, and though admittedly these constitute but a pale reflection of his work, I doubt that it is a deceptive one. Jackson has never come to this country, we know him only through recordings; yet I should like to show that, although the approach through records may not be entirely adequate, we can rely on it for the essential. We won't follow Jackson's development step by step, nor attempt to compare the early stages of his career with his music as it is now. I feel that an over-all appreciation of his music would be the best possible introduction to a more significant analysis of a single, highly representative piece; but, in order for this analysis to *be* more significant, we must learn to examine each and every facet of a work.

One may wonder exactly how Jackson's music assimilated the qualities he acquired as he went along. Did some sudden awareness determine the selections and rejections inherent in this development? Did Bags' style evolve under the pressure of outside influences, or were these influences merely grafted onto some unreasonable impulse from within? These hypotheses are all credible, but none can be verified. All we can know for sure is what Jackson's records tell us—that from 1945 to 1947 his gifts were still inconsistent and unassertive whereas only a few years later they were firmly established.

The Milt Jackson of the Modern Jazz Quartet has found himself as an artist; this is why his early recordings no longer satisfy us. Bags' early work was a deceptive indication of his future development. (A musician of whom this can be said seems lucky indeed when one thinks of all the jazzmen whose early performances have been betrayed by their recent work!) The deceptiveness of those early records was due not so much to their defects as to what their very content seemed to portend. For though at the beginning of this article I wrote that Jackson has kept his early promises, this is not quite correct. Jackson has, it is true, gone on to produce a body of extremely interesting works but their basic qualities are not what we were led to expect. Bags has taken a new tack and it is rather difficult to detect any musical relationship between his recent and his early work. When he began playing the vibraphone, his style was rather dry, metallic, and aggressive, deliberately lacking in charm; today his instrument has a limpid, ethereal, at times almost disembodied sound, as though he had the power to make us forget the impact of the mallet on the bars, to absorb it completely. His chief defect used to be a certain insensitivity to rhythm which made even his most successful improvisations seem a bit stiff. In his days with Gillespie he confined himself, in medium-tempo pieces, to a long-short phrasing based on triplet figures which seriously cramped his swing. Dizzy's own fondness for very fast tempos often led Jackson out of his depth; the resulting tenseness disrupted the flow of his music which would dissolve into set recipes and clichés. Milt seems to have eliminated these dangerous tempos from his repertory. His style has gained in self-assurance, his phrasing has become suppler and better ventilated; in a slow tempo he will even make very free use of different rhythmic values; all these things attest to a fresh orientation of his aesthetic conceptions which would have been impossible without an extraordinary increase of rhythmic sensibility. Moreover, Bags has managed to resolve the conflict between excessive harshness and excessive sentimentality that once hampered his style; today he is a perfectly balanced artist.

Among the recordings which best sum up Jackson's progress between the ages of twenty and thirty, the most significant is *Delaunay's Dilemma* (Modern Jazz Quartet, 1953). His simple statement of John Lewis's delightful theme is, in itself, a sign of true mastery. The sensibility underlying this precise, relaxed, straightforward performance, free of any extraneous effects, is marvelously adapted to the emotional content of the melodic line. Jackson takes the syncopated notes in his stride; he treats them very smoothly, almost gently, making no attempt to accentuate them, thus giving added relief to the Parker-like accentuation he later applies to them in his chorus. These two approaches to syncopation constitute the opposite ends of Jackson's wide expressive range, each aspect of which is associated with one of the great eras of jazz. Though Bags came to jazz in the stormy days of bop, he was not oblivious to the appeal for greater purity made by Miles Davis and the other leaders of the "cool" movement. Many of the components of his present style derive from earlier forms of jazz, however. For while his melodic language has become both suppler and more rigorous, he still uses melodic blues figures similar to those he used ten years ago; and while the long-short construction has fortunately gone out of his rhythmic vocabulary, the triple division of the beat remains in the form of the triplets that are frequently slipped in between two groups of eighth notes. But despite these occasional technical similarities, Jackson's work in *Delaunay's Dilemma,* partly because of the new musical context, was conceived in a completely different spirit from *Oo Bop Shbam* or *Confirmation.*

The triplets with which Jackson so often separates groups of eighth notes may be his way of combating the monotony so easily engendered by an eight-to-the-bar medium tempo. But, if so, this rhythmic device (of which Jackson seems fonder than any soloist I know; in fact it may be regarded as typical of his style) falls somewhat short of its mark. In the long run this constant alternation between double and triple time-values is almost as monotonous as an uninterrupted flow of eighth notes. When Bags is in the mood to swing he has no difficulty enlivening his delivery and diverting our attention from a faint stiffness of phrasing. But this stiffness is accentuated whenever Bags is not up to par; at such times his technical competence is not enough to hide a certain lack of "vital drive" which, in a musician of his caliber, may be regarded as a shortcoming. This may be why, even though he has shown his aptitude for swing on a great many occasions, I cannot go along with the musicians and critics who feel that Jackson "swings it" as well as his famous predecessor, Lionel Hampton. In my opinion, the swing that Hampton could produce in medium tempo has yet to be equaled.[22]

Yet Jackson does not lack rhythmic imagination, far from it. He often ventilates his phrasing with long note-values (i.e., *Moonray*), accelerates his delivery by doubling, or more subtly, by slipping a few sixteenth notes into a framework of eighths (i.e., the opening break in *All the Things You Are* with the Modern Jazz Quartet). At other times he devises highly unusual rhythms, like the riff made up of four equal values for three half-beats which occurs in *Stone Wall* and at the beginning of the second chorus of *Delaunay's Dilemma*. The displaced repetition played toward the end of his long solo in *Ralph's New Blues* (Modern Jazz Quartet) may also be regarded as a form of riff.

Modern jazz thrives on the notion that a variety of rhythmic figures is more conducive than the riff to that relaxed type of swing—much sought after since its introduction by Lester Young—because the relentless repetition of the riff ultimately becomes an element of tension. Jackson is abreast of his time and doesn't overwork the riff; in fact his recorded work hardly contains more than three or four choruses in which he resorts to this formula. One of the most noteworthy examples occurs in *La Ronde* (Modern Jazz Quartet, Vol. 2); here the recourse to the riff, coming after the stop-chorus of the interlude, is intended to restore a sense of balance.

Like a great many improvisers Bags frequently resorts to set melodic figures. Even Parker, for all his incomparable melodic inventiveness, had his favorite figures. Jackson's are less original and sometimes, when his imagination runs short—as in the bridge of his solo in *On the Scene*—they lead him to resort to a whole string of melodic clichés, so that he sounds, for a moment, like any run-of-the-mill jazz-man. Only for a moment, however, for there is much evidence of his superior melodic imagination, for example, the re-markable melodic continuity of his chorus in *All the Things You Are* (Modern Jazz Quartet) in which he develops—unconsciously, I expect—the quotation from Parker's ver-sion of this piece which appears in the last bar of the state-ment. Or consider the unusually intelligent transition, around the twelfth measure of *Heart and Soul,* by which he shifts from an ornamental statement of the theme to a variation on it and the continuity of style between this variation and the faint ornamentation used in the first part of the state-ment.

The first sign of this superiority is, of course, his choice of notes with repect to the basic harmony. Bags seldom makes the mistake of so many vibraphonists—I have Hampton in mind, especially—whose instrument seems to induce them, for no apparent reason, to break the chord down into endless series of arpeggios. Jackson's melodic line is thoroughly con-junct, but does not exclude broken chords by any means (those triplets of his are often arpeggioed, especially when they occur on the off-beat). Moreover, the analysis of a solo such as that in *Eronel* (with Monk) proves that Milt knows how to blend diatonic and chromatic scales intelligently within a single phrase.

Jackson's loveliest solo in medium tempo (a bit slower than medium, actually) occurs, without a doubt, in *Django* (Modern Jazz Quartet). After the statement of the theme —in which he participates *mezzo voce*—Milt attacks his double chorus with a brief ascending phrase, played in anacrusis—five or six notes embodying all the impetuosity of his quivering sensibility. After this dazzling attack—which alone would make this piece worth listening to—Bags goes on to improvise at length on the unusual structures of John Lewis's theme. His masterful, flawless improvisation is free of redundancy and teeming with melodic ideas, some of them very fine. As for the phrases he plays in the pedal point section, the fact that they may have been arranged rather than improvised in no way detracts from Milt's qualities as a soloist. If he improvised them, so much the better; but even if they were written for him, how can we help admiring the skill with which he incorporates them into the fabric of his solo? Then too, Jackson's rhythmic vocabulary is richer here than usual. His use of "irrational" time-values in the first part of the solo gives the phrasing an impulsive turn which faithfully reflects, I feel, one of the most attractive sides of his personality.

2

Until now I have limited my analysis to Jackson's work in medium and fast tempos; in so doing I have deliberately neglected the most captivating side of his production. For there is no doubt but what his best recordings, from the 1948 version of *You Go to My Head*—his first major achievement—to the recent *All of You,* belong to the area of slow jazz, more specifically to that of the ballad. The tempo has often enabled Bags not only to reach the peak of his talent, but to rise head and shoulders above every other vibraphonist. We need only compare *What's New* or *Milano* with any of Hampton's famous versions of *Stardust* to see how far Jackson has outstripped his illustrious predecessor. When Milt stands behind his instrument and starts to concentrate, drawing forth those impalpable tones which he assembles so skillfully, there is no need for some stagehand to turn a red spotlight on him; the Jackson mood develops all by itself, and is perceptible, I am told, to the most inexperienced listener. Never having heard Bags in person is not a serious handicap here, since the great vibraphonist's extraordinary presence comes across even on records.

In stating the theme of a ballad, Milt is generally quite scrupulous; once he has chosen a theme, he respects its general contours (his themes, it is true, are usually selected in function of this attitude). He is conscious of the beauty of his tone, and is fond of letting long note-values reverberate freely. He even seems to draw them out for added plasticity, as Miles Davis does; Bags uses different means, of course, but he has similar aesthetic aims. He gives the impression of listening to his own sound, not complacently, but as though under a spell; when the melodic progression forces him to leave certain notes before they have stopped reverberating he seems to do so with regret. Sometimes these notes last so long that they finally clash with chords in the piano (i.e., the statement of *I Should Care*). Judging by the way he draws them out, Jackson actually seems to delight in these strange dissonances.

In themselves, however, these long values are not enough to form the woof of a coherent musical fabric. Milt fits them into a delicate system where they are held in place and interconnected by brief figures, short scales, or barely

sketched chromatic runs. Fairly often, the resultant structures are linked together and commented upon by more
dynamic phrases (i.e., *Lillie*). One of the finest examples of
this device occurs in *My Funny Valentine,* on a descending phrase that ushers in the last few measures of the statement. Bags also uses it to "embellish" the statement in
his splendid version of *Autumn in New York* (recorded
with the Modern Jazz Quartet in 1953); here he employs phrases which, though reminiscent of Parker, are
played in a cooler mood, without the countless little asper-
ities that the Bird would have added. Stresses are rare but
violent; Jackson has learned to make the most of the *sfor-
zando* (or sudden increase of volume), and the wide spacing
of these blinding flashes further emphasizes the great refine-
ment of his playing.

I hope that this attempt to describe Jackson's slow statements has not given the impression that his conceptions are a
bit traditional nor cast doubts on his powers of development.
For while it does seem that Bags has a well-defined notion
of the ballad and that his capacity for invention is not un-
limited, the fact remains that both are much broader than
I have been able to convey. A comparison between two solos
recorded in the same year (1951) should suffice to show the
extent of Jackson's range; for what could possibly be further
from the Davis-like intimacy of *Yesterdays* than the fiery,
Parker-like volubility of *'Round About Midnight?*

There are a number of very respectable jazzmen who,
though they manage to create a climate during the statement of a theme, seem unable to sustain it when they must
plunge into an improvised chorus immediately afterwards.
We need fear nothing of the sort with Bags; once the Jackson mood is established, the chorus simply blossoms forth,
as though it had found its natural element; the soloist seems

to drink in the atmosphere he has secreted, drawing from it the very substance of his improvisation. This is where Jackson shows his greatness as a jazzman. Whether he doubles the time before reverting to the phrasing of the statement—as in *The Nearness of You*—or whether he makes clever use of the ambiguities arising from the fact that drums and bass are beating different tempos—as in *My Funny Valentine*—both of these impromptu inventions undeniably grew out of the mood created by the initial long notes. Less frequently, Milt seems to run through the whole statement with a detached, indifferent air, as though saving his strength for the chorus. Thus, his solo in *Milano* has an explosive effect. After a very restrained statement of the theme, Jackson soon gives free rein to his lyrical temperament in spinning clusters of thirty-second notes which provide a sharp contrast with the straightforward eighth note phrases of the theme. The musical tissue begins to expand and bristle with *sforzandi* which lend unexpected sharpness to its contours. Then the phrasing is organized in terms of double time; the values become more even, with a preponderance of sixteenth notes, but the tissues remain varied, rhythmically fluid, and beautifully articulated.

3

Jackson's recordings of *Autumn in New York* and *Milano* are without doubt highly representative of his style and creative powers. There is just one record of his which goes, I feel, even further, attaining an exceptional aesthetic level which Jackson can probably reach only on his very best days; this is the 1952 version of *What's New*,[1] which I would rank among the loveliest slow solos in the history of

---

[1] I am referring to the version recorded with J. Lewis, P. Heath, and K. Clarke, before the actual founding of the Modern Jazz Quartet.

modern jazz (obviously only recorded improvisations or compositions may be regarded as part of jazz history).

From the very first measure of *What's New*, the listener falls under the spell of the Jackson mood, here greatly enhanced by the proud, elegant patterns of John Lewis's piano, Kenny Clarke's quivering brush work and the muffled beat of Percy Heath's double bass. Milt sets forth the opening phrase in octaves—played pianissimo—and ends it with a "commentary" in the form of a sixteenth note break introducing the change which the theme undergoes starting from the ninth bar. Now the octaves give way to delicate embellishments on the theme which are *not* purely decorative; rather, they comment upon the melody from which they sprang and to which they remain tightly bound. This approach does not make the thematic statement heavy or choppy, as sometimes happens with the ornamental runs, always in the form of arpeggios, of which certain pianists are so fond; on the contrary, it elucidates the theme, bends it to the soloist's own conception as he sizes up and reshapes the original phrase, putting the stamp of his personality on it.

The bridge—introduced by a splendidly played, riotous thirty-second note break à la Parker—is handled in a similar, though less dynamic vein. An increasingly lively phrasing prepares the way for the return of the tonic and the reintroduction of the main motive; during the break in measures 23 and 24, the phrasing suggests double time with extraordinary rhythmic freedom and flexibility, attaining a glorious climax in the high notes. One splendid invention consists in delaying the long-awaited return to the tonic ever so slightly, as though Bags were sorry to let such deep-felt tension resolve itself; and yet this tension was meaningful only because it was bound to be relieved. From the point of

view of lyrical inspiration, no Jackson record has ever surpassed the infinitesimal moment of ecstasy coincidental with
the sound of that slightly overdue tonic. This is one of those
moments of exceptional beauty peculiar to jazz and unthinkable in any other art form. Indeed only the relative freedom
of the soloist with regard to his rhythm section and the fact
that both are dependent on the framing of the chorus make
it possible for us to appreciate the full implications of this
delay.

How could Bags resist the temptation of letting that tonic
sing out in all its purity, alone, immaculate and as though
motionless, defying time for a fraction of a second while beneath it the tireless piano still spins out a countermelody?
The piano seems to embody this new found repose but also
to challenge and even negate it by disturbing syncopations.
Lifted from its context, this tonic note would have nothing
to distinguish it from those which begin each of the other
three periods in the statement, except that it is in a higher
register. It is neither longer, nor more heavily stressed than
they, yet it has a completely different meaning, for it constitutes both a deliverance and a gateway to a world of
fresh sensations. Though occurring in the middle of the statement it is already the end of that statement and rules out the
possibility of a balanced ending for the thirty-two bar theme
(in other words, an ending similar to the beginning). Bags
was clearly aware of this imperative arising from his own
playing; after a brief attempt to return to the theme (bars
26 and 27), he departs from it deliberately and drowns the
melody in a flood of thirty-second notes which, without actually prefiguring the improvisation that follows, seem to
announce its coming. This melodic effervescence is asymmetrical with respect to the phrase's pivotal tonic and its

intense movement actually serves to offset the feeling of motionlessness suggested a moment earlier.

For the next sixteen bars, Jackson adopts double time, improvising his variations in a spirit of ever-increasing rhythmic freedom. Am I wrong to feel that he is more at home in these false tempos than in the true medium or fast tempos, that double time is in close keeping with his individual sensibility and provides the best possible outlet for his sense of swing? None of Bags' medium tempo pieces give us the feeling of perfect rhythmic sway and complete ease conveyed by the break in divided tempo which leads up to the last phrase of *What's New*. It is a pity that while this break is the most swinging passage in the piece, it is the weakest from a melodic standpoint. Actually, this weakness is due to an unfortunate resemblance between this break and its counterpart in the exposition. It repeats a musical idea already expressed sixteen measures earlier, and though Bags may have been obsessed by the idea of a fullblown effusion in the high notes, the effect is, of course, less rigorous than before; the listener does not experience again that unique moment in the first chorus, so that the use of a long tonic here seems little more than a trite repetition of the theme.

This redundant passage has scarcely subsided, however, before Jackson brings in a new element of feverish lyricism and low-keyed vehemence; this is expressed in successive, shifting phrases that no longer "breathe" at all but seem to be rushing toward a desperate end in a series of waves that constitute a splendid conclusion. In this brief passage, Bags comes close to Parker in his moments of greatest pathos. The overwrought quality of the passage is the sign of an approaching explosion, and indeed the solo is suddenly suspended on a descending seventh. After that, everything returns to normal; Bags takes up the theme again and follows it with a coda which, after such an authentic burst of lyricism, may seem conventional. True, it does not display any of the exceptional sensibility that transfigured the coda of *Autumn in New York*, but it does perform a useful function, creating the climate of abatement necessary both to bring the work to an end and to justify it. Here Jackson chose to sacrifice the possibility of attaining even higher summits of delirium in favor of an organic structural discipline. (The danger of prearranged codas in improvised jazz is that one never knows what frame of mind the soloist will be in when he has to readjust to the set patterns.)

4

It remains for me to situate Milt Jackson with regard to his contemporaries. He has come in contact with the greatest modern jazzmen and recorded with a good many of them. His first experience with Gillespie, though by no means negligible, cannot be placed on the same level as his contacts with John Lewis and Thelonious Monk. For, without knowing him personally, I would venture to say that Jackson simply must have a great pianist at his side, that his rarefied style must be sustained by a thoroughly articulate counter-melody and that his melodic line needs the support of strange or sumptuous harmonies.

On the various occasions when this support has been provided by Monk, it also became a challenge. Such an angular accompaniment, with its harmonic eccentricities, undoubtedly bothered Milt now and then (this would seem to be the case in *Criss-Cross*); at other times, the challenge referred to above is probably more a conflict of style (in *I Mean You*, for example, the vibraphonist's conjunct style contrasts strongly with the pianist's frequent changes of register).

In other pieces, however, they managed to achieve profound understanding. After all, one of Jackson's first important recorded improvisations was *Mysterioso,* recorded with Monk in 1948; Bags begins his chorus with ornate, circuitous, choppy phrases full of incidentals, which seem to reveal a secret affinity with Monk's own aversion to an obvious continuity in the musical fabric. Jackson's solo in *Epistrophy* is another example, not of his adaptability—I don't think he *is* that adaptable—but of his keen perception, for it must not be an easy task to play with Monk. This chorus holds a place apart in Bags' recordings, less because of the ambiguous tonality and disjointed character of the accompaniment, than of the way in which the soloist rises to this twofold challenge, finally extracting from it the substance of one of his most astonishing solos.

Still, there is no doubt in my mind but what John Lewis is the ideal partner for Milt Jackson. In a short article on the Modern Jazz Quartet, A. Lundberg implied that only the group's commercial success kept Bags from leaving John. If this is so, then Jackson's desire to regain his freedom can only be motivated by his boredom with the quartet itself. The combination devised by John Lewis may not suit Jackson's aspirations; the Modern Jazz Quartet's repertory may not be to his liking. And yet if there really is an aesthetic conflict between the musical director of the Quartet and his vibraphonist, I doubt that this conflict could affect the relations between soloist and accompanist. On many occasions Jackson and Lewis have demonstrated their perfect musical understanding; I believe that Bags is too much of a musician not to have a proper appreciation of the exceptional intelligence and sensibility of the great accompanist that is John Lewis. What other pianist could have given him the support he needed in *What's New* and ten other ballads they recorded together?

One may wonder whether the portrait of Milt Jackson that I have tried to infer from his recordings is really accurate. We will be able to tell when Bags finally comes to Europe, as we have been hoping he would for so many years. My opinion of certain aspects of his talent may surprise some musicians; they may even be in contradiction with Jackson's own aims. Am I wrong to feel that he has attained greater mastery in the slow ballad than in the medium tempo blues, wrong to appreciate him for the mood he excels in creating rather than for his swing, wrong to rank his sensibility and capacity for lyricism above his melodic gifts? Perhaps. Yet this is the image I have formed of him after a long and careful analysis of his chief recordings.

CHAPTER 15

A Rebirth of the Ellington Spirit

A Tribute to Gil Evans

"A composer's critical writings are primarily a critical analysis of someone else," writes Pierre Boulez. "Between technicians, bluffing is scarcely feasible; no fool's bargain can compensate the observer's frustrations and disappointments."[1]

Is this observation by the well-known French composer applicable to jazz? If so, perhaps it will serve to justify the reservation which, despite my enthusiasm for Duke Ellington's contribution to jazz, I cannot fail to have about his current work.[23]

I feel I may say that my admiration for the many superb records made by the Duke in the past is second to none, and that few musicians have benefited more by his conceptions than I have. But though at times I am still impressed by the Duke's orchestra, the scores it has been playing for the past

---

[1] Pierre Boulez, "Probabilités Critiques du Compositeur" in *Domaine Musical,* Grasset, Paris, 1954.

ten years seem unworthy of his former musical accomplishments (though I do not know to what extent he is really responsible for them). Are we about to see other composers take up where the Duke left off? The fact that the Duke was so far ahead of his contemporaries for so long was undoubtedly responsible for his limited influence; now, however, I feel that this influence is coming into its own.

Few arrangers have, as yet, realized the importance of Duke Ellington's legacy: at least one of them, however, has sensed it very deeply; his name is Gil Evans. Eight years after *Boplicity*, seven years after *Moondreams*—these figures are a disgrace to the world of jazz—Evans was commissioned to do a series of arrangements for a Miles Davis album. In the meantime, everyone had forgotten who he was; jazz people don't give much thought to anyone who doesn't sing, play the trumpet, or lead a band. Gil's friends were a bit uneasy; what was going to come out of this second encounter between those two masters of cool jazz, the soloist Miles Davis, and the arranger Gil Evans?

The scores were written and recorded in the spring of 1957. To accompany Miles, Evans employed a large orchestra composed of five trumpets (including Ernie Royal) four trombones (including Frank Rehak and Jimmy Cleveland), two French horns, one tuba and four reeds and woodwinds (including Lee Konitz) and a rhythm section with Paul Chambers and Art Taylor. This record has now been released under the title *Miles Ahead*.[2]

It is destined, I believe, to have very great repercussions, even though it has had a rather lukewarm reception. Those who feel that nothing counts today except the funkiest of blues find Evans's concepts outdated (these are often the same who, five years ago, were clamoring that the blues

_____

[2] Columbia CL 1041.

was "out of date"). Others feel that while the arrangements are conceptually admirable, they have been distorted by an illusory "faithful" performance. I, for my part, wish that Evans's musical idiom took greater account of the blues spirit, and we may be sure that he himself would have liked to see his arrangements rehearsed as often as necessary and even performed publicly a few times before they were recorded. Now and then there are still a few rough spots, if not actual flaws, to be heard; a few solos were post-recorded—never a desirable procedure in any case—and it would have been well to replace one or two musicians (the flutist, for example, whose phrasing in *The Duke* shows that he simply does not understand the score). But even the sum of these reservations is of little weight compared with the amount of imagination, inspiration, and sensibility that went into a record which, with all its faults, constitutes a remarkably successful achievement.

I'll wager that if Duke Ellington has had a chance to listen to this record, it made him very happy. After so many years the Ellington spirit has come into its own again, with a persuasive power it has never known since Ellington's own masterpieces of 1940. For the first time since then we are presented with a consistent approach to the full jazz band. Intentionally or not a great many passages on this record constitute a tribute to the great Duke. I shall cite only a few examples: the aural texture of the backgrounds in *My Ship*, the rhythmic texture of those in *The Maids of Cadiz*, as well as the band finale of *Don't Wanna Be Kissed*. As for Brubeck's pretty tune, appropriately titled *The Duke*, I can only repeat what Quincy Jones has said of it: "Gil put Duke into *The Duke*." No plagiary is involved here, of course, merely a filiation which is, in the last analysis, an honor to Miles and Gil, since an artist reveals himself in his choice of sources. Moreover, these arrangements are full of original inventions and their sumptuous sonorities are constantly controlled by an unfailingly keen ear. Gil Evans can write music, there is no doubt about that! I know of no other jazzman who can compare with him as harmonizer and orchestrator, though he may not have quite come into his own as a composer. His own *Blues for Pablo* is the weakest piece on a record in which all the other themes chosen are unusually fine; but then perhaps it merely seems so weak because it does not go with the rest of the pieces. It was originally meant to be recorded by Hal McKusick's small ensemble, and Evans was probably wrong to include it in a set where it was bound to be out of place. This mistake is emphasized by Evans's use of an interesting formal innovation; he has grouped the ten pieces on this record into one long suite, the coda of each piece becoming the introduction to the next; despite a succession of highly contrasting tempos, the unity of style is so great that one can easily forget about the composers of the various tunes used (Brubeck, Davis, Kurt Weill, etc.) and think of the whole as a single composition to which *Blues for Pablo* does not, I feel, really belong. In this respect Evans, though strictly speaking an arranger rather than a composer, nevertheless succeeds in appropriating the composer's prerogatives and in making an effective contribution to jazz form, as the Duke did in his greatest works.

On this record Davis brilliantly confirms what we already knew: that his gift for lyrical expression is greater than that of any modern jazzman. But whereas the lyricism of Charlie Parker bordered on frenzied rapture, that of Miles tends toward a kind of ecstatic trance. This is most appreciable in slow tempos, and indeed his loveliest solos in this album are to be found in the ballads (though Miles also applies his inimitable detachment to the medium tempo piece *Miles Ahead,* and in *New Rumba* turns out a particularly successful stop chorus). In a slow tempo, Evans's own lyrical temperament reinforces that of Miles; witness the exposition of *My Ship.* The discreetly soaring quality of the theme may be said to prefigure the transformation it is about to undergo with the entrance of the ecstatic Davis flügelhorn. Similarily, the impalpable background accompanying his solo is like a projection of Miles' own state of introspective contemplation. The collaboration of Davis and Evans is even more convincing in *The Meaning of the Blues* and *Lament;* here the soloist employs all the wiles of his allusive trumpet, and the band's rare interjections constitute the direct expression of what Miles only hints at.

Gil Evans is capable of filling the vacancy left by Duke Ellington. He is by far the finest arranger of his generation. And insofar as there can exist an ideal arranger for Miles's splendid trumpet, then Gil Evans is the man!

CHAPTER 16

Monk or the Misunderstanding

Nietzsche provided a subtitle for his book. It is: "A Book for Everyone and No-one." "For Everyone" does not, of course, mean for each one in the sense of just anybody. "For Everyone" refers to every person insofar as he is truly human and to the degree that he is reflective of the root of his being. "... and No-one" means not for those curiosity seekers who gather from everywhere, intoxicate themselves with isolated bits and passages taken out of context and become dizzy from the book's language, half-singing, half-shouting, sometimes thoughtful, sometimes turbulent, often lofty and occasionally flat—instead of committing themselves to the train of thought which is seeking here its verbal expression.

—*Martin Heidegger*

1

The world of jazz is a stage on which it matters less what the actors say than the way they say it.[24] Conviction, rather than creative genius, is the key to success, whether it be the artificial—or simulated—conviction of a rock 'n' roll star, the sincere conviction of the crack rhythm and blues expert, or the absolute conviction of a musician who has only his conviction. For the crowd's need to be convinced is the nose by which it is most easily led. The millions of addlepates who cheered Hitler on the eve of the second World War were expressing and sharing an absolute conviction; many of them died before they could realize that their enthusiasm reflected nothing more than abysmal feeble-mindedness.

In other words, it matters little that you have nothing to say, so long as you say it ardently and artfully. The best method of convincing an audience whose average mental age is under twelve is to comply with that norm yourself. If you happen to have the intellect and sensibility of an adult— even those of a backward adult—a shadow of a doubt, something resembling a conscience is likely to creep into your mind and that will be the end of your capacity for expression. If ever you lag behind your audience for a fraction of a second they will slip from your grasp and pass judgment on you. In that fraction of a second they will see how ridiculous you are; never again will you be able to restore the sacred ties that held them at your mercy.

Conviction, then, is essential on both sides of the footlights, as is that clear-cut propensity for intellectual vacuity which, as everyone knows, is the most obvious sign of acute musical gifts. So now the stage is set; the curtain is ready to rise on a play the plot of which must, of course, be "simple and direct." This is the magic recipe which jazz critics have been using for the past thirty years to designate, for the benefit of admiring crowds, the *ne plus ultra* in jazz. But tradition grows richer with the passing years. In highly cultured periods such as ours, new concepts may be brought to light, and indeed, today that prime aesthetic virtue, *facileness*, has found a place among the basic values. In order for music to be good it must be simple to understand; after all, is it not meant to be enjoyed by the greater number? There are, however, a few counts which still leave room for improvement. For example, judging by their audience-participation reactions,[1] newcomers to jazz seem to be having greater and greater difficulty assimilating certain rhythmic elements; the *afterbeat*, in particular, seems to constitute an insoluble problem for them. May I therefore suggest that we simplify jazz rhythms, which are definitely becoming too complicated. By doing away with the afterbeat, by rehabilitating the Sousa approach to accentuation, jazz would unquestionably win over those thousands of men and women of all ages who, like the characters in the *Grand Illusion* or Céline's Bardamu, are fascinated by military bands. Moreover, that perplexity which sometimes besets the lone hand-clapper in a side balcony would give way, for the greater good of public morals, to the joys of unanimity fully achieved at last. One! Two! One! Two! What could be more simple and direct than this language, so dear to the heart of every true-blue Frenchman?

Have the pleasures of irony led me astray from reality? I wish this were so. I wish that a hideous march in the form of a blues had never been cheered by a large crowd, satisfied at last in its craving to identify, if only for a moment, its own national folklore with the highly touted music of the Negro. On the other hand, I hope that a particularly respectful salvo of applause will one day greet the presence on a Parisian stage of such a true artist as Thelonious Monk.

Now Monk is neither simple nor direct, he does not al-

---

[1] One characteristic of the fanatic is his *desire to participate.* In jazz, this participation takes the form of hand-clapping.

ways say what he has to say as well as he might and the
things he has to say are subtle, seldom easy to grasp, and not
at all meant for the enjoyment of the greater number; his
rhythmic notions go far beyond that afterbeat which some
find so elusive, and yet, by one of those paradoxes common
to jazz, if ev r we are lucky enough to hear him in Paris, he
will probably reap the same wild cheers that have marked recent performances given by great, not-so-great, and mediocre
jazzmen alike. I'll even bet he has a good box office take.

Only yesterday Monk was a has-been, a half-forgotten
page in the history of jazz. Today he is an established value,
with a label and a price tag. A single article was all it took
for everyone in France to grasp the significance of the new
Messiah, and it wasn't even a real article, just a hasty discussion over the tape recorder of *Jazz Hot*.[25] The next
day everyone swore by Monk and Monk alone. Not so long
ago he couldn't even find work and now he is vying with sea-
side charmers and Granz's circus stand-bys for the top berths
on opinion polls. The musician who once terrified us all no
longer seems to disturb a soul. He has been tamed, classified,
and given his niche in that eclectic Museum of Great Jazzmen which admits such a variety of species, from Fats
Domino to Stan Kenton. Only a man like Miles Davis has
the courage to fear Monk: "I like the way he plays, but I
can't stand behind him. He doesn't give you any support."

Thelonious Monk is not a great classic, one of those musicians who, like Armstrong or Parker, attracts impressive
crowds of disciples. Monk is a man alone, disturbing and incomplete. In the eyes of history he may be on the wrong
track; but this, perhaps, is what most endears him to me.
He is the solitary man who, when he looks back, does not see
his fellow travelers—who doesn't even know if he has fellow travelers. A few years ago, I thought his example would

be irresistible; today I am not so sure. The enticements of facileness, the sense of security that lies in numbers, the love of success and the cult of the dollar may, in the end, prove stronger than the strange aesthetic vertigo which a few people experience on hearing some of Monk's fiery outbursts.

Monk may not have gone far enough yet. His music may not yet be sufficiently well-developed to exert any lasting influence on the majority of musicians. One wonders how much attention the young jazzmen of the forties would have paid to Charlie Parker had his music not been so thoroughly accomplished. Moreover, the desire for change is not nearly so widespread now as at the end of the war. The situation today is more like that of 1940 than of 1945. But then perhaps the contrary is true. Perhaps Monk, without even realizing it, has already gone too far on the path he has chosen; for it is a path which must inevitably lead to that complete divorce between jazz and popular music prefigured, I feel, in the shocks periodically inflicted on jazz by the few artists who have managed to divert it from its original course (and these shocks have been increasingly violent: the Bird was a less "popular" musician than Lester, Lester less than the Duke, and the Duke less than Armstrong). If this hypothesis is correct, we may expect to see any attempts to propagate Monk's conceptions thwarted by a powerful inertia on the part of both public and musicians. Monk is fashionable now; let him make the most of it! Before long he may again be as neglected as he was on his first visit to France, for there is reason to fear that his present success is based on a sad misunderstanding.

Snobbery does not in itself explain Monk's popularity, which is fairly limited in any case. True, his music probably does provide the snob with almost as good an opportunity for intellectual bullying as the Modern Jazz Quartet's.

John Lewis fans like to refer to Vivaldi, Monk's may drop the name of Webern. But there undeniably exist music lovers who are sincerely fond of his work, for Monk has that power of conviction without which, as we have seen, it is impossible to crash the gates of success; his is certainly not as great as that of an Erroll Garner or even a Horace Silver, but he does have it. And even those who confess that Monk's music disagrees with them have to admit that it does not leave them indifferent. Moreover, his music may benefit by the aura of strangeness created by the scintillation of a thousand bizarre details which add color to the clear-cut structures of a basically traditional language. If Monk's music were no more than the alloy of bizarreness and security which many think it is, it would seem insignificant indeed alongside that mad, delirious tempest that the Bird, in his greatest moments, sent sweeping across the valleys of jazz. The Monk craze cannot last unless it be strengthened by the difficult exploration of the real Monk. Is such a thing conceivable? Each of us must provide his own answer to this question in the light of his personal experience. Not to mention the sense of dread that the outwardly rather monstrous appearance of Monk's world inspired in me for so long, I found that in order to begin to grasp its deeper meanings I first had to come up with solutions, and, above all, come to grips with problems similar to those suggested in his work.

For there is something else.

Monsieur Dumesnil[2] would be very surprised to learn that a semiliterate Negro is capable of conveying, through a musical idiom which he would peremptorily regard as highly primitive, beautiful ideas that are both thoroughly musical

---

[2] I am referring to René Dumesnil, the scholarly musicologist of *Le Monde* who will, I hope, forgive my using him here as a symbol of that useless criticism which has an exact counterpart in jazz.

and truly modern, ideas which his favorite composers, whose "achievements" he periodically hails with that leveling pen of his—I am referring to men like Florent Schmitt and Henri Tomasi—would be quite incapable of even conceiving.

"Ideas that are *modern* and *musical*"; does this mean that Monk is not a true jazzman? After all, the true jazzman is not supposed to overstep the bounds of his art, venturing onto the arid steppes of serious music or, worse still, the glacial plains of the twelve-tone row. But here we may rest assured, for no twelve-tone sirens have lured Monk away from jazz. He probably doesn't even know that such music exists. I can safely say that the gradual development of his language has been the result of intuition and intuition alone. Those who debate as to whether or not this language is still part of jazz are simply quarreling over words, and I prefer not to join them. I feel that although Monk's sonority and his system of attacks and intensities are highly personal, they are definitely in the tradition of jazz. Even his opponents acknowledge the rhythmic precision of his playing and the great power of the swing he produces. It is rather hard to apply the word "funky" to Thelonious's music and for this reason some may deny that he is a great blues musician. I do not agree, however; I feel that on the contrary, his stroke of genius consists precisely in having applied a fresh treatment to the blues theme, making a renewal of its inner structures possible without any distortion of its style (always perfectly intact in his music).

The fact that this true jazzman and eminent blues musician, whose improvisations are free of any academic formalism, should display such overt concern with *form per se,* ought to provide the reader with food for thought. Contrary to the belief of certain naive observers who prefer to deny the existence of aesthetic problems rather than come to grips with them, jazz is not generated spontaneously. It is the work of human beings, of a special kind of human being called the artist. Now the nature of the artist, in contrast with that of the mere musician, amateur or professional, is to be dissatisfied. This feeling of dissatisfaction is a basic, permanent, and inexorable force in the artist, compelling him to upset the equilibrium achieved by his creative predecessors (and sometimes, in the case of the very great, by the artist himself). The truth of the matter, as seen by any objective historian, is that jazz, born during the decline of Western civilization, has made contact with that extraordinary concept of musical form which made it possible for Western music—or at least its masterworks—to rise above all the art forms of any known civilization. This is where one may expect the stalwart champions of "pleasurable music" to arch their backs and bare their claws. For is not this notion of form the beginning of the end? If jazz is that happy, fun-making music they love and which satisfies their appetites, then anyone who isn't satisfied is wrong. Monk is wrong. In the eyes of these people, *who do not feel that the absence of form is a deficiency,* the very idea of form is necessarily parasitic. Its entrance into the world of jazz constitutes the rift in the lute. But the worst is yet to come, since the existence of form calls for someone to organize it, someone who thinks music, in other words, that personification of evil, the composer![3]

I am not afraid of being contradicted on this point, I *know* that I will be, and loudly so. When conservative critics are out to combat a new idea they invariably find ten musicians (and not necessarily bad ones) to defend their theor-

---

[3] The reader is requested to refer to Chapter 9 which contains a summary distinction between the composer, the arranger, and the tune or theme writer.

ies. This time we may expect them to find a hundred, for the subject is an important one. I will not lose any sleep over this, however, since even a hundred musicians who are blind to the necessity of form cannot prevent the existence of a Thelonious Monk. However, in order to forestall a useless flood of well-meaning protest, I must be more explicit. When I say that the absence from jazz of a certain dimension that I call form is a deficiency, I do not mean that jazz is now entirely devoid of form, but that form does not play a vital, active role in it.[4]

The pioneers of jazz borrowed from Occidental folk music a sense of symmetry and the principle of regularly recurring structures. With these ideas as a starting point, jazz, like every other form of music inspired by Occidental folklore, grew up according to a fixed, stereotyped, formal principle which stopped developing almost entirely once jazz ceased to be folk music. In the meantime, the notions of symmetry and continuity in musical discourse were being destroyed by Debussy, Schönberg, Stravinsky, and Webern, and replaced, in the works of the major contemporary composers—Barraqué, Boulez, Stockhausen—by a completely different conception. If a twelve-tone score like *Séquence* or *Le Marteau sans Maître* bears as little resemblance to a classical symphony as a Klee abstraction does to a Corot landscape, it is because the world of music is now based on the notions of asymmetry and discontinuity. Thelonious Monk is to be hailed as the first jazzman who has had a feeling for specifically modern aesthetic values.

2

The danger threatening the author of an article like this—which is not meant to be one of those "surveys" conducted

---

[4] Certain works of Ellington are among the rare exceptions to this rule.

at a respectful distance but a very personal essay, an attempt at "subjective" analysis—lies in the fact that he is constantly tempted to alter the course of reality, insidiously shaping it in the image of his own wishes. I must continually guard against painting an ideal picture of Monk; it would be as unfaithful and as inadequate as the portrait for everyday use which we have already rejected. Monk constitutes a splendid promise in the world of jazz; we must not make of him a false Messiah.

Monk, as I have already said, is incomplete, and must be taken as he is. How could I seriously claim to see his work in its ultimate perfection? Do I have the right to look over his shoulders, to look into the future with his eyes—for would they even *be* his eyes? Would they not be mine, jaded by their contact with contemporary art, hampered by a cultural background which, in this particular struggle for insight, may not be the right weapon? These scruples may seem out of place, yet the reader had to be informed of them, for they constitute the very substance of the form of commitment I have chosen. If critical analysis is to be regarded as a creative act, then it must be conducted with that same rigor which characterizes, I feel, the work of art. In a field where pure speculation can so easily assume the guise of established truth, we cannot legitimately tolerate any retreat into the realm of imagination.

Monk has occasionally disappointed me. Not that I have ever regarded him as more advanced than he actually is; it's just that no one can be expected to maintain those positions of extreme tension which define the creative act. Is there any man, any artist, brave enough to hold out against the tremendous weight of the tradition from which he sprang and the pressure of the milieu to which he belongs? Then too, it is just possible that what I take for a yielding on his part is actually a sign of renewed effort. Those ballads that Monk, in the solitude of his apartment, plays over and over again may be leading him through secret channels toward some unexpected explosion. Close though he may seem to the origins of jazz—"I sound a little like James P. Johnson," he says, not without a touch of irony—we suddenly find his tremendous shadow stretching out across those ill-defined regions where the stride piano is but a memory and where the notion of steady tempo, which is at the very root of jazz, seems to have vanished.

It is not hard to see why I am so fascinated by his remarkable *I Should Care* on the record called *Thelonious Himself*. It consists of a series of impulses which disregard the bar line completely, pulverize the musical tissue and yet preserve intact that "jazz feeling" which so readily evaporates in the smoke of a Tatum introduction. These elongations of musical time, presented here in a "non-tempo" context, are probably the direct descendants of those "in tempo" elongations to which his famous solo in *The Man I Love* (with Miles Davis) had already accustomed us. Is it so unreasonable to think that they exist as a function of a second, underlying tempo, imperceptible to us but which Monk *hears* in all the complexity of its relationships with the figures he is playing?

One may wonder what remains of the theme of *I Should Care* after this acid bath, and, in fact of the ballad in general, considered as an essential element of jazz sensibility. Personally, I am delighted at this transmutation, which is in keeping with the breath of fresh air brought to jazz, in my opinion, by his own original themes. Will Monk's concepts abolish at long last those "standards" with which every great jazzman since Armstrong has carried on an exhausting and, despite an occasional victory, perfectly fruitless struggle?

Will he supply the Lester Youngs and Charlie Parkers of the future with new themes that will constitute a loftier challenge to their talents? Yet hardly has this hope been uttered, than Monk himself dashes it by rehashing a theme as insignificant as *Just a Gigolo* (though, again, this may not be the retreat that it seems, but simply one more assault on that fortress where great treasures lay hidden).

Are we dealing with the return of the prodigal child, exhausted by his travels, or the obstinate—though perhaps hopeless—labor of the gold digger who never says die? This is the only alternative to be deduced from Monk's constant and disconcerting seesaw motion. For it goes without saying that I refuse to accept the intermediate hypothesis, whereby a man who has upset the very fundamentals of the jazz repertory is really satisfied with these degradingly insipid popular songs. If this were true he would have followed the examples of Garner and Tatum and sought a wider choice of melodies for, as it has often been remarked, his is unprecedentedly narrow.[5] In recording sessions and public performances, as well as in his own practice periods, Monk plays the same pieces over and over again. We may find his choice of tunes surprising, not so his desire to limit himself, for it is one of the most characteristic channels of expression for his basic feeling of dissatisfaction.

It is Monk who first introduced a sense of musical time

---

[5] Not only do Garner and Tatum accept the legacy of ballads and "standards," they actually welcome it with open arms. Monk, on the other hand, does keep his distance, though often succumbing to the temptation of decorative arabesque in the form of awkward and conventional arpeggios. (Cf. Gunther Schuller's essay on his records, *The Jazz Review,* November, 1958.) One wonders whether these figures, practically nonexistent when he improvises on his own themes, do not indicate the inward discomfiture of the least "decorative-minded" of all jazzmen in the face of material whose very impurity cries out for decoration.

into jazz; the interest of this new dimension does not, how-ever, lie solely in its foreshadowing the destruction of a thematic lore to which the vast majority of jazzmen—and their public, as well—still seem very much attached. Of course, this battle is worth waging—and winning. Some may miss *But Not for Me* or *April in Paris* the way others will miss *Honeysuckle Rose*; their sentimental attachment to a tradition blinds them to the fact that these very tunes are the most damning evidence against that tradition. The real problem, however, is situated on a higher plane; the reper-tory question is merely a necessary, though attenuated re-flection of that problem, which is to determine whether or not form—I haven't lost sight of it—can become an active ingredient of the jazzman's poetic universe. Musical time is one of the two main props sustaining this notion of form; the other is musical space. And Monk has revolutionized musical space as much as musical time.

Let's look at Monk's accompanying technique. Is Miles Davis right in saying that he doesn't give the soloists any support? Would it not be more accurate to say that he gives them a new kind of support, which jars with the more tra-ditional notions of Miles, but which might be capable of stimulating the improvisational gifts of a less self-assured soloist? Referring to his collaboration with Monk at the Five Spot, John Coltrane has said: "I learned a lot with him. . . . It's another great experience."[6] If we are to believe Bobby Jaspar, who says that Monk and Coltrane "attained the highest summits of jazz expression," the two musicians must have gotten along fairly well. Personally, however, I must admit that I have never heard any soloist (except per-haps Milt Jackson) who wasn't bothered to some extent by

---

[6] August Blume, "An Interview with Coltrane," *The Jazz Review*, January, 1959.

Monk's approach; nor can I easily conceive of a soloist to whom Monk's accompaniment would be *indispensable* in the way that Roach's was to Parker.

Indeed, Monk brings to his accompaniment a concept of discontinuous musical space, which I have yet to find in the playing of either Coltrane or Rollins. Making the most of the piano's specific qualities, he has built his accompanying style on a system of isolated or contiguous note-groups which contrast with one another through sudden changes of register. The mountains he pushes up, the valleys he hollows out cannot, of course, pass unnoticed. Yet Monk is not trying to show off or create an illusion of orchestral accompaniment. Even while seeking to *free himself of the soloist,* Monk's ultimate goal is to exalt him anew by enveloping his melody with an aura of polyphony. The assistance given soloists by the discreet vigilance of the traditional accompanist, whose only concern is to clarify tricky harmonic passages, always results in a pedantic formal subservience; because of their close interrelationship, both parts are subjected to the strict rules of a hierarchical system which allows for no value inversions whatsoever. Thus, ever since the end of the New Orleans era, improvised jazz has deliberately confined itself within very narrow limits, the very limits from which even Italian opera, despite its formal poverty, managed to escape from time to time: accompanied melody considered as the only possible form of musical discourse. Monk's sudden jumps from one register to the next constitute a far more drastic attempt at transcendency than previous devices (such as that of dividing a chorus into shared four-bar sequences the way modern jazzmen do). The soloist's supremacy has been challenged at last but Monk has gone even further than that; his technique restores to jazz that polyphonic fabric that was once so important, through the new notion of discontinuity. This twofold contribution may greatly complicate the task of future soloists, but jazzmen have already shown that they were capable of rising to challenges of this sort.

Similarly, while this conception of accompaniment implies a promotion of the accompanist, it also makes great demands on the musician who accepts it. Continual changes of register do not automatically make one a genius; these changes must be the expression of an interior vision which must, in turn, derive from a keen insight into musical space and time. Ten years of mediocre row music have taught us that discontinuity can, at times, be nothing better than an alibi for incoherence. If Monk's conceptions win out, it will be much more difficult to be a good accompanist in the future. Monk himself is a great accompanist—or more precisely a *great background organizer*. He has a marvelous gift for measuring the weight of a given dissonance and the density of a given attack in order to combine and place them at that precise point in musical space where their impact will be most effective, relative to the length of time he intends to hold the note and, above all, to the length of the surrounding silences—in other words in function of a subtle space-time relationship which no jazzman before him, not even Parker, had ever experienced in all its urgent beauty.

Once this is established, it matters little that Monk is not, as some say, a great harmonist, in the usual sense. Anyone who is bent on destroying all those insipid ballads with their attractive chords must agree to abandon most of that harmonic cast-off. The pretty passing chord with its Ravel-like savor nearly killed jazz; I say let it die, and good riddance! Monk is accused of depersonalizing the chord; I say more power to him. He is also accused of establishing, in his own themes, a system of extreme dissonances, which is likely to invade jazz as a whole. This may be so, but it may also be the only condition under which he can rejuvenate the conflict of tension and repose, shifted by him from the domain of harmony to that of registers.

Though by and large Monk's solos are less daring than his accompaniments, occasionally they are far more so. The solo idiom enables him to play a dominant role in the form of the collective work, shaping it in terms of that basic choice between symmetrical and asymmetrical structures. Prior to Monk, Charlie Parker had already brought a certain melodic and rhythmic discontinuity to jazz, but in order for this idea to have germinated in his work the Bird would have had to reconsider his highly traditional approach to the set pattern. Such a reappraisal would undoubtedly have led him to a new form of structural equilibrium. Within more modest limits, Gerry Mulligan did have the courage to transgress this basic notion of the set pattern, but his innovation belongs to the composer's rather than the improviser's domain; it was probably more accidental than deliberate, and did not deeply affect the basic substance of a musical vision still governed by the notions of symmetry and continuity.

If one examines separately Parker's discontinuity and Mulligan's unorthodox patterns, Monk may seem less advanced than they, but this is a mere optical illusion. Only in Monk's music do asymmetry and discontinuity enhance one another, thereby assuming their full, symbiotic significance. This symbiosis is highlighted successively by each of the other components of a language which, though not yet thoroughly coherent, is nevertheless sufficiently well-formed to have already given us glimpses of the role that formal abstraction can play in jazz (as in the *Bag's Groove* solo).

The principle underlying Monk's chief structural contribution is one of brilliant simplicity. The incorporation of shifting, asymmetrical structures into a symmetrical type of fixed "combo" structure constitutes an obvious, though partial, solution to the problem of form in jazz—so obvious in fact that I am surprised no one ever thought of it before. Monk made no attempt to escape from the closed circle of the twelve bar chorus; he simply reorganized it along less baldly "rational" lines. In other words, he has done for jazz structures what two generations of musicians before him had done for jazz rhythms. There is a very fine analogy here between, on the one hand, the play of rhythmic tension and repose stemming from the arrangement of figures and stresses with respect to a permanent tempo, and, on the other, that formally static—or kinematic—situation resulting from the symmetrical or asymmetrical balance of a set of secondary structures within a fixed primary structure. Compared with the rhythmic concepts of Chick Webb, those of Kenny Clarke constituted a decisive step toward asymmetry and discontinuity; this forward leap created a gap which has been filled at last by Monk's comparable advance on the level of form.

True, this is only a partial solution to the problem; the structural conflict devised by Monk does not suffice to establish the over-all formal unity of a piece. Other than the style, the only unifying elements in his music are unity of tempo and key, a unified range of timbres and an over-all sequential framework;[7] these constitute a foundation that is far too weak to sustain that deep, inner life-beat which we know to be the highest and most secret form of musical expression.

The chief problem facing the creative jazzman today is, to my mind, that of *capping the piecemeal unity that has been achieved on the structural level with a true, organic unity.*

---

[7] By *sequential* I am referring to the succession of chords constituting the framework of a chorus, or of part of a chorus.

There are two ways—and it would seem, only two—of reaching this still distant goal. One may be called thematic; it implies a constant effort on the part of the improviser to remain in contact with the original theme, as he infers from each new variation a whole set of fresh material intimately related to both the theme itself and the various transformations it will have undergone on the way. According to a recent essay by Gunther Schuller, Sonny Rollins has succeeded in making important progress in this field (which Monk has not disdained to prospect, either).[8]

I must confess, however, that I cannot share this eminent critic's enthusiasm for the thematic approach as conceived by Rollins. The large proportion of his solos devoted to ad lib playing compared with the brevity of the thematically connected sections, inclines me to feel that, despite the appreciable results obtained by this outstanding saxophonist in these thematic passages, thematic improvisation is a delusion to be avoided. Several centuries ago this field was opened to the investigations of the individual composer, and I expect that it should remain his domain. The improviser is most likely wasting his time in attempting to appropriate it. A soloist with an extraordinary memory (and a thorough mastery of composition) might conceivably improvise fifteen or twenty choruses and still remain strictly thematic, in other words take account of all the various intermediary situations arising on the way. But in a less utopian perspective, I am afraid that the thematic approach can only sterilize jazzmen's sense of improvisation. If they are at all concerned with rigor they will gradually be led to "crystallize" their solos, so to speak. Many will probably regard the thematic approach as a mere recipe with which to fill the gaps

---

[8] Gunther Schuller, "Sonny Rollins and the Challenge of Thematic Improvisation," *The Jazz Review*, November, 1958.

in their imagination, while the others will behave like the water-carrier who, for lack of a magic rod to strike forth fresh springs along her path, must continually return to the same well.

One may wonder whether a thematic revolution in jazz would have much point today, when the thematic approach is vanishing from serious Western music. I would never claim, of course, that jazz can take a short cut to that arduous, esoteric realm from which the very notion of theme is banished. It is completely unprepared for such a jump, and I do not feel, in any case, that jazz, which is tonal and modal by nature, need seek its salvation in that direction. The search for formal concepts peculiar to jazz is a special problem for which jazzmen must find a special solution. Monk's solution, though related in some ways to the formal conceptions of serious modern music, is not indebted, for its guiding principle, to any school of music, past or present, which is foreign to jazz; this, I feel, is essential.

His solution seems to have grown out of a number of obsessions which crop up in recordings done during the fall and winter of 1954. The most famous of these—*Blue Monk* and *Bag's Groove*—have a strange kinship; it is as though the first were a prefiguration of the second. *Blue Monk* contains nearly all the structural elements which were to serve as a basis for the idiom of *Bag's Groove*; if it seems less "pure" than the later solo, this is because its structures are not correctly situated with respect to formal space and time. Monk's solo in *Bag's Groove* constitutes, to my knowledge, the first formally perfect solo in the history of jazz. With it was born the notion, to my mind primordial, that a space-time dialectic is possible in jazz, even when it is weighed down by symmetrical superstructures and their rigid, apparently ineradicable, tonal foundations. This *unique* achievement of Monk's goes to prove that, above and beyond the traditional "theme and variations" (or rather "sequential variation") a musical tissue can renew itself indefinitely as it goes along, *feeding on its own progression* as it leaps from one transformation to the next. This concept, which may be called "open form," is both thematic and "athematic"; it constitutes an unexpected illustration, through jazz, of the existentialist axiom, "existence precedes essence," and is admirably suited, by its very nature, to that "spur of the moment" art form which is musical improvisation. Moreover, I am convinced that some of the best choruses of the great improvisers of the past already contained the embryo of a notion which was left to Thelonious Monk to bring to light. The key to this emancipation seems to have lain in his earlier discovery of the catalysing effect that asymmetrical structures can have on symmetrical ones.

This contribution could not, however, lead him directly to that supreme realm of musical form where the very existence of a work of art—a collective work, in any case—is determined. Still, his contribution as a bandleader is very appreciable, if less revolutionary than some of his achievements as a soloist.

Roger Guérin has given us the following description of the formula used by Monk last summer at the Five Spot in almost all the pieces played with his quartet: after the statement of the theme, the tenor would take a great many choruses, accompanied only by bass and drums; then Monk would gradually worm his way into this trio and the increasing density of his accompaniment would rapidly lead the tenor to conclude. Monk would now go into his main solo; after a few choruses, however, his playing would tend to grow gradually sparser until it became the background for a bass solo; the piece would end with a restatement of the theme, preceded only occasionally by a solo on the drums. Compared with the usual succession of choruses, this form, which may be regarded as a jazz equivalent of the "tiling process" first used by Stravinsky in the *Rite of Spring* (the piano "covering up" the tenor only to be "covered up" by the double bass) represents an immense forward stride. The weakness of this procedure lies in its invariability, for when applied to a group of pieces it becomes a *mold* and constitutes a reversion to the aesthetic level which Monk had surpassed with such mastery in *Bag's Groove*.[9] Monk's sense of form has not yet been extended to the band per se and though an extraordinary theme writer, and a unique improviser, he may simply not have the means to do so. The realization of the all-encompassing formal concept implicit in his ideas may have to await the intrusion into jazz of that foreign species, the composer.

The scope and gravity of the problems raised in this chapter, the reappraisal of jazz as a whole which they imply, plus my own awareness that I have proposed only very partial solutions to them, make it, I feel, unnecessary for me to enter as deeply as I might into the minor facets of this great musician's gifts. It is generally agreed that Monk periodically lapses into the errors of his youth, that he resorts to facile piano tricks, and is not a great keyboard technician. But then Art Tatum was a great keyboard technician, and look what he did with his virtuosity! Even that cruel, sarcastic humor of Monk's, though it has real depth, is, in the last analysis, merely an incidental aspect of his musical temperament.

I like to remember that one of the great composers of our time, a man who can hardly be accused of any indulgence for

---

[9] Monk's ensemble records do not belie Roger Guérin's account, though they do not always corroborate it.

jazz, once listened to the *Bag's Groove* solo with an ear that was more than merely attentive. Disregarding the tiny technical defects, he immediately grasped the meaning of the acute struggle between the disjunct phrasing and those pregnant silences, experiencing the tremendous pressure that Monk exerts on his listeners, as if actually to make them suffer. When the record was over, just one remark was enough to compensate for all the rebuffs that the mediocrities of jazz had made me suffer from his lips; it was made in connection with the F sharp that follows a series of C's and F's in Monk's first chorus, and which, for all its brevity, constitutes one of the purest moments of beauty in the history of jazz. "Shattering," was my friend's only comment.

The recorded works of Parker and even Armstrong are probably more substantial and more consistently successful than the erratic and restricted music of Monk; yet there are moments, fleeting though no doubt they are, when Monk rises to summits which neither Armstrong nor Parker, in their records at any rate, ever managed to reach. It is not unthinkable that in the eyes of posterity Monk will be THE jazzman of our time, just as Debussy is now seen to have been THE composer of the period immediately preceding the first World War. I am not in the habit of making predictions, but I will say that I would be deeply happy if this one were to prove correct. It is always possible that Monk himself would not recognize the portrait I have drawn of him here, and that I have merely deepened the misunderstanding that I wished to dispel. Let us hope, however, that beneath an outer skin which to some seems rough and dry, and to others delightfully provocative, I have managed to reach the core of that strange fruit which is the music of Thelonious Monk.

Part Five

Listening Notes

CHAPTER 17

Commentaries on Five
Improvisations*

1. Charlie Parker's solo on *Ornithology*

The melodic elegance of this solo, the classical purity of
its construction, and its rich rhythmic incidentals—together,
of course, with Parker's excellent performance—go to make
it one of the loveliest alto sax choruses ever recorded. In the
number from which it is taken, this solo comes immediately
after the statement of the theme. Parker is accompanied only
by the rhythm section. In this connection I must point out
that for certain passages I have replaced the chords that
Dodo Marmarosa plays on the record with slightly different
ones which, I feel, are more in keeping with the soloist's improvisation; thus in measure 14, I feel that the passing chord
is an indispensable complement for the melodic line devised
by the Bird (Fig. 8).

From the standpoint of melody, this solo's chief characteristics are the way in which Parker alternates broken chords
with conjunct phrases and his elegant avoidance of tra-

* See Appendix note [26].

Fig. 8

ditional melodic cadences in phrase endings (he does not play the fundamental, except in measures 7 and 8, where the harmony in question is, in any case, a transition rather than a phrase ending, since the chorus is divided in half, "16 plus

16"). But it is mostly for its rhythm that this chorus deserves a detailed analysis. All I can do here is to point out the way in which accents are distributed so as to occur now on the beat (measures 3, 5, 12, 13), now on the offbeat (measures 1 and 14), now before the beat (measures 9, 10, 11, etc.). One should bear in mind the importance of these accents, as well as that of the "suggested" notes (in parentheses in the illustration) without which the solo would seem rather flat. Rhythmically speaking, the outstanding passage is that which extends without interruption from bars 16 to 20 (neglecting, therefore, the double bar at the end of measure 16); in it a cell consisting of a displaced rhythm (measure 16) is expanded, so to speak, by the addition first of one, then of two note values (measures 17 and 18).

Two last points worth noting are: the similitude between the ascending figures with which three of the solo's phrases begin, in measures 9, 21, and 24 (this may be regarded as the solo's only flaw); and the typically Parkeresque "ventilation" of the melodic fabric by means of long rests in measures 4, 8–9, 13–14, 20–21, 23–24, and 27–28.

REFERENCES:
Record number: Dial LP 201 (out of print).
Recorded on March 28, 1946, Copyright by Charlie Parker.
E flat alto saxophone. The transcription is in the instrument's key.
Metronome: ♩ = 244

2. Dizzy Gillespie's solo on *I Can't Get Started*

This was Gillespie's first recorded version of Vernon Duke's famous theme. It seems to be one of the great trumpet player's favorites, for he plays it in concert. He even follows the general outlines of the original version in the introduction and coda, doing most of his improvising during the statement of the theme (this is not so strange as it seems, since he only plays one chorus). The statement is generally accompanied on the saxophones with a counter-melody which was to become the opening theme of *September Serenade*; for the sake of simplicity I have omitted it from my transcription of this chorus. Similarly, I have had to leave out a number of rubatos which, if taken down as played, would have been rather hard to read (Fig. 9).

In any case this solo is less interesting rhythmically than it is harmonically and melodically. As early as the fourth bar of the introduction, Dizzy makes use of the opposition between the third (G♯) in the accompanying chord (E 7) and the G natural which he plays as an appoggiatura of its ninth; this relationship turns up again in bars 30, 40, and 42. The solo is full of diminished fifths (measures 7, 14, 15, 22, etc.) which serve to make the melody tense and even tortured. Other points worth noting are: Dizzy's use of chromatic passing chords in measures 19–20 and 35–36, the gradation in measure 26, the alternation of conjunct melody and arpeggioed chords (generally involving some further embellishments as well, such as the eleventh which occurs in measure 32), the frequent use of ornamentation (grace notes) and the over-all medium tessitura.

The high point of this improvisation is undoubtedly its famous coda (which Gillespie incorporates into other solos of his, and especially the introduction to *'Round 'bout Midnight* in which he improves it considerably by leaping a ninth at the end of each period, in place of the rather banal second which turns up here in measures 40 and 42). I should point out that this coda impinges, so to speak, on the chorus proper, shortening it by two measures.

Fig. 9

REFERENCES:
Record number: Columbia CL 1036.
Recorded in January of 1945, Copyright by Vernon Duke.
B flat trumpet.
Metronome: $\downarrow = 58$

3. Django Reinhardt's solo in *Solid Old Man*

This is generally felt to be one of the loveliest guitar choruses on a slow blues. Accompanied only by the bass and a soupçon of drums (a combination which foreshadows the Mulligan Quartet), Django improvises a completely free melodic variation: nowhere is it related to Rex Stewart's riff-theme. Django even takes advantage of the piano's absence to make an intelligent departure from the harmonic framework of the blues, by "minorizing" the subdominant in bar 2.

His melodic handling of this solo is remarkable in every respect. Its outstanding feature is the wealth of appoggiatura that it contains; the first note is one example and the blue note at the end is another. Bar 4 is particularly revelatory of Django's fondness for appoggiatura; they follow each other in quick succession, hiding the simplicity of the actual melodic fabric, which is based on the plain statement of a B flat chord. Needless to say the passing note, when it has a short value, plays only a secondary role in this ornate style. However, if one places "parentheses" around the three groups of identical ascending notes in bars 5 and 6, the A flat in bar 6 turns out to be a passing note despite the apparently disjunct context. Here again, Reinhardt displays great cunning in dissembling a musical idea which, without this device, might seem overly bald (Fig. 10 .

The construction of the chorus provides another source of interest. The history of recorded jazz contains few solos

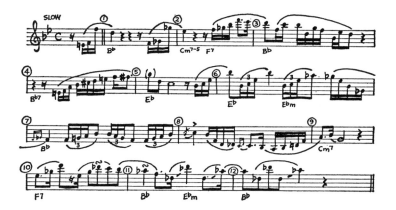

Fig. 10

displaying such "asymmetrical balance." Thus the first phrase, composed of three anacrusis groups, leads to a rhythmic termination in the tonic chord (bar 3). The first two groups are obviously symmetrical, but the third (end of bar 2) is rhythmically displaced and melodically embellished. Yet the relationship between the three is clear, since each begins with an ascending minor second. The series of appoggiatura in bar 4, constituting the anacrusis of the second phrase, is also based on a minor second. This second phrase, which ends on the first beat of bar 7, is particularly interesting rhythmically. Django works out a series of rhythmic variations on a single melodic figure, first expressed in sixteenth notes, then in triplets, and finally in displaced triplets. The third phrase extends through bars 10, 11, and 12 of the chorus. In the last two measures it boils down to an alternation of blue notes (remarkably exploited for their melodic and expressive qualities), preceded by a preparatory pattern in which D flat (bar 10) is given a special "intonation," as though Django wished it to take on a particular significance; actually, it serves to announce the final blue notes.

Thus the curious construction of this blues involves three phrases, divided as follows: 1–3, 4–7, 10–12. What happens between the first beat of the seventh measure and the first beat of the tenth? Does Django stop playing? Not at all; these three measures contain a fairly long phrase, which *does not belong to the solo proper*. It is part of an orchestral type "accompaniment" which Django "heard in his head" while playing his improvisation. The "parenthetical" character of this phrase should be apparent to every attentive listener.

REFERENCES:
Record number: Capitol TBO 10226.
Recorded on April 5, 1939, Copyright by Rex Stewart.
Metronome: $\downarrow = 72$
A guitar will actually sound an octave below what is indicated here.

4. Sarah Vaughan's chorus on *Mean to Me*

The version of this song discussed here was issued by Columbia. It comprises a vocal statement of the theme, a half-chorus on the tenor sax and a final vocal chorus; it is this chorus which I have transcribed here (Fig. 11).

Of all the great female jazz singers, it is Sarah Vaughan, perhaps, who takes the greatest liberty with the melody and rhythm of a theme. She brings off better than anyone else that modest tour de force which consists of adapting the original words to a new melody.

Sarah's rhythmic imagination is at least the equal of her

Fig. 11

melodic inventiveness. For while, in many respects, it belongs to a very common variety of paraphrase (measures
12 and after; the bridge, etc.), elsewhere it involves a
free variation form that is so bold as to seem almost instrumental.

In fact I have had to simplify a number of figures which,
written out exactly as they are sung, would be difficult to
read. The motif in measures 14 and 15, for example, is sung

with a slight "lag," which becomes so great in measures 16 and 17 that I had to take the opposite tack and write down each note as I heard it (whereas the rhythmic plan would seem rather to suggest a form of syncopation, a full eighth note in advance, the A flat falling on the beat, as it does in measures 18 and 19).

The obligation to sing the words keeps Sarah fairly close to the AABA structure of the theme. Yet the transition from the first phrase to the second is quite remarkable. After a long, syncopated repetition of an "embroidered" dominant (measures 6 and 7)—sung with a maximum of swing—she "changes gear" on the first beat of measure 8 and, after a short arabesque, hits the highest note of the passage (on the first beat of measure 9) then dives brusquely into the low register (a device which is vocally very effective). Thus the transition between the two phrases is brought off with great elegance, reminiscent of Miles Davis's best constructed solos. To achieve this, Sarah did not shrink from a rather distorted delivery of the text.

Mention should also be made of the coda (measures 33 to 36) which is almost entirely chromatic and seems—though this is only an illusion—to take Sarah to the top of her range with the high E flat that occurs at the end of the chorus forming a major ninth with the tonic.

N.B.—The harmonic figuring in this transcription has been deliberately simplified.

REFERENCES:

Record number: Columbia CL 745.

Recorded on May 19, 1950, Copyright by Roy Turk and Fred Ahlert.

Metronome: ♩ = 120.

5. Eight measures of Billie Holiday

The early jazz singers, who specialized in blues, rarely took advantage of the improvisational spirit which was already developing among instrumentalists. The earliest examples of vocal jazz were characterized by a scrupulous respect for the original theme. Only much later did vocalists undergo the influence of improvisers and begin to transform tunes. I hardly need to point out that it was Louis Armstrong who was chiefly responsible for this liberating step, when he applied his experience as an instrumental improviser to scat singing and interpretive vocalisation.

Was Billie Holiday the first female singer to have profited by Armstrong's example? I cannot say so for sure, as I am not familiar enough with her immediate forerunners. It seems fairly certain, however, that she represents a significant stage in the history of vocal jazz. From a melodic standpoint, her contribution is twofold, concerning both variations and embroideries on the theme. Now and then her achievements constituted valid extensions of Armstrong's and laid the groundwork for the modern vocal style which has reached its full development in the work of Sarah Vaughan.

There is no question of my doing a survey of Billie Holiday's main recordings in this short essay. For this reason I prefer to limit myself to the examination of a single piece, and in fact only to a few measures of it; after all, I am bound to make myself clearer by concentrating on just one point. As the subject of my analysis, I have chosen the first few measures of *These Foolish Things*. This example will enable me to draw an interesting parallel with Lester Young's famous recording of the same theme.

Billie Holiday has often been compared with Lester. A

number of critics have even said that the President borrowed a great deal from Billie and that today's cool style actually originated in her singing. This may be so, though I feel that the affiliation is not so obvious on the conceptual level as on those of timbre and sensibility. Billie's paraphrasing sticks close to the Armstrong tradition, which was the point of departure for her revolutionary effort. In trying to define the exact nature of this effort, we shall also see that a comparison between Lester's and Billie's melodic conceptions does reveal an unmistakable kinship.

First let us look at the accompanying transcription (Fig. 12). The middle staff contains the melody of *These Foolish*

Reprinted by permission of Estate of Eleanora McKay a/k/a Billie Holiday.

Fig. 12

Things in its usual form; the top staff contains the beginning of Billie Holiday's paraphrase on this theme while the bottom one contains the beginning of Lester Young's; all three have been transcribed in the same key: E flat. Needless to say these simple transcriptions make no pretense of *expressing* either Billie's or Lester's actual interpretations. They are simply meant to record their *melodic* elements for purposes of comparison.

One thing is apparent at first glance and that is both soloists' rejection of the original melody. All too often jazz themes are selected on the basis of their popularity, obliging the jazzmen to struggle with unbearably trite melodies of which *These Foolish Things* is an excellent example. When this happens the musician has only one alternative: either improve on the theme or forget about it. Classical jazzmen's respect for the theme as such generally led them to adapt, like Louis Armstrong, the first solution. We need only examine the first eight bars of Lester's solo to gauge the progress made since then. Lester has no qualms about *replacing* the original theme with a different melody which, in the beginning at least, cannot be regarded as a variation, since the only relationships between the two are purely harmonic. This daring lack of respect is thoroughly justified; the great beauty of Lester's new theme is undeniable, and is a far cry from the wishy-washy, facile banality of the original.

Billie Holiday's solution is a compromise. She starts off with a frankly different melody; her first two measures are as far from the original as Lester's. She too found it impossible to sing the melody as such, she too gives up any hope of "improving" it. So far their methods are identical. Gradually, however, the theme begins to make itself felt, allusively at first (measures 3 and 4) then more and more openly; it seems to be taking shape again note by note. Notice how intelligently the singer uses this process of gradation. By the seventh and eighth measures all doubt has vanished; even without the words, the song would now be easily recognizable. This is not the case with Lester's solo, in which only the harmonic framework recalls the source of his improvisation. Personally, I prefer the greater "purity" of Lester's conception, but there are two elements which argue in Billie's favor. In the first place, she has to deal with the words and there is no doubt but what these always tend to draw singers back to the original melody; the instrumentalist's freedom is infinitely greater. And in the second place, this first phrase of *These Foolish Things* happen to end better than it begins; Billie may be said to have a valid musical reason for gradually coming to terms with the theme as she leaves the ugliest part of it behind her.

The first four measures of our example show that Billie Holiday's melodic imagination involves a certain economy of means. To lead up to the dominant B flat in measure 4—which is the first melodic resemblance between "her" theme and the original—she makes use of only three notes (C, D, and G).

This extreme melodic sobriety pays off in the fifth measure, when she reaches the high F which is the highest note in the phrase; because it appears only once, this note takes on special importance. It is worth noting that Lester reaches his highest note (high C) only a half-beat before this very same point; what is more, he endows that same high F with a special rhythmic and expressive value, so that its role is similar to the one it plays in Billie's version. There are other points of comparison between Lester's and Billie's melodic concepts: the conjunct quality of their first bar (in which both melodies double back on themselves); Billie's skip of a fourth (G to C) in the second measure which turns up in a slightly different form in Lester's third and fourth measures; the fact that in both solos the lowest note is a low C which first occurs in the fourth measure, etc.

This very brief and fragmentary analysis was designed merely to draw the reader's attention to certain features of Billie Holiday's melodic style. Obviously this goal, modest though it is, could be reached only in so far as the example chosen was a good one. There is, I feel, an extensive and absorbing study to be done on the melodic relationships between the work of Holiday and Young; I have only been able to touch on the problem in these few lines. I hope other investigators will be able to carry on with it.

REFERENCES:

Lester Young—
Record number: Imperial LP 9181.
Recorded in October, 1945, Copyright by Bourne, Inc., ASCAP.

Billie Holiday—
Record number: Verve MG V-8338–2.
Recorded in March, 1952, Copyright by Bourne, Inc., ASCAP.

Part Six

Prospects of Jazz

CHAPTER 18

Popularity or Recognition?

The problem of public recognition of an art form provides an excellent subject for psychological and sociological analysis. We do not know much about the growth of that "society of the intellect," to which Marcel Proust refers in connection with Beethoven's Quartets, nor about the nature of the laws governing the relationships between a work and its intended audience. Our knowledge is even less when it comes to jazz, since the milieu in which that music develops has never been rigorously studied, either.[27]

Caught up in the whirlwind of its constant transformations, jazz decays almost as soon as it comes into existence. By the time a jazzman has begun to grow tired of his own music, age has already deprived him of his creative powers. Fortunately, a fresh cell immediately appears to replace the dying one; it is in the nature of young, vigorous organisms to transform themselves constantly, from within. But the public, in its satisfaction with time-tested forms, may be out of phase with the changes required by the artist. This phenomenon has been frequent in European art, ever since the time when the greatest Western artists found it necessary to challenge the popular bases of art (a challenge which was embodied in the most significant works of Rembrandt and J. S. Bach long before Nietzsche, Mallarmé, Cézanne, and Debussy laid the premises for a "modern" art whose essence is in no wise popular).

A work of music may be "popular" in either of two ways: by its origins or by its audience appeal. These do not always coincide. A pure product of popular art is sure to fall upon sympathetic ears within the society that gave it birth, but may find an audience in other social groups only at the price of its aesthetic integrity. The way in which the samba has been watered down in the United States and Europe is one example among hundreds of this process of degradation. It is also possible for a truly aristocratic work, like Chopin's E major *Etude,* to be adapted and simplified, and its meaning thus altered, to comply with "popular taste" which despises expressive refinements; but here, too, the work's essential message is lost on the way. More generally speaking, works conceived in a serious cultural perspective are unlikely to become popular without first having to go through a kind of purgatory from which some reputed "difficult," never emerge.

For a "difficult work," true popularity consists in being *recognized* by a reasonably numerous elite. It is this "cultural" path, necessarily a long one, which has led to the consecration of the most famous masterpieces. An artist and his work can only attain recognition through the influence of a few clear-sighted minds; those who come under this influence, will in turn transmit it to a larger group. At times this chain reaction may come to a halt; but if the artist has real genius and his work is really great, it will soon resume its course. I have no doubt but what Hermann Broch will in time be recognized, just as Dostoevsky was; but it is unlikely that *The Death of Virgil* will ever be as popular as *Gulliver's Travels* or *Madame Bovary*.

Setting aside any concern with "folk purity" in the ethnological sense, the most convincing standard of popularity lies in a given musical product's capacity to satisfy the immediate needs of a wide audience, while the least deceptive criterion of recognition is our being able to qualify that product as a *work*; in other words, it must be sufficiently rigorous in its conception to affect those whose sensibility has been shaped by contact with the works of great artists, past and present. These two criteria are well worth applying to jazz, as they establish hierarchies which help to clear up a good many situations. Tommy Dorsey, whose silly diatribes against modern jazz are best forgotten, was popular for a long time but never had any serious recognition. On the other hand, Thelonious Monk, who is recognized today as one of the most important figures in the history of jazz, is not yet really popular. The two jazzmen who have best brought off the tour de force of being both popular and recognized are Louis Armstrong and Duke Ellington; yet a close analysis of their output might reveal a certain oscillation between rigor and facileness—Ellington's *Ko-Ko* as against his *Caravan,* Armstrong's great lyricism as against his crowd-pleasing antics—which, if it turned out to be a constant factor in their work, might well be seen to have diminished the significance of the tour de force.

Moreover, Ellington's and especially Armstrong's music was still very close to those popular origins from which jazz has since gradually freed itself. Both won popularity before anyone was aware of the cultural interest of jazz. And it is only fair to add that they were largely responsible for the recognition of jazz as an art form; in fact this recognition coincided with the recognition of *their* music. During the

202 / *Toward Jazz*

blissful period that followed, commercial success seemed to be the inevitable recompense for artistic quality, though the contrary was not always true; the best records of the Benny Goodman Quartet, Teddy Wilson, Lionel Hampton, Fats Waller and Count Basie all sold well, and even Coleman Hawkin's *Body and Soul* was a best-seller. At the time no one dreamed that a great jazzman could fail to be popular.

Only with the coming of modern jazz did the problem of "how to be popular" really arise. The bop revolution, which suddenly introduced a "new way of experiencing jazz," dismayed the public. Despite the encouragements of propagandists, who unfortunately were better skilled at juggling words than defining them, the crowd returned to the more accessible forms of music (which were also easier to dance to) once it had satisfied its curiosity. For having tried to invent a complex idiom, capable of accounting for certain aesthetic truths, jazzmen found that theirs had become a specialists' art; by cutting their music off from its popular origins, they deliberately limited their audience to a group of connoisseurs. It now became difficult to achieve popularity without forsaking the achievements of modern jazz. Since the end of the war only a very few jazz musicians—and not always the best—have managed to find favor with the general public who, in any case, prefers the howling idols of rock 'n' roll.

The era of the great stars seems to be over; we should have no regrets. After all, it is far more comforting to see that Charlie Parker, Dizzy Gillespie, and John Lewis have, each in his own way, carried jazz a bit further along the road to recognition. Today a great jazz soloist is not very likely ever to be understood by the public at large, and very unlikely ever to reach a social status comparable to that of the principal bandleaders of the twenties and thirties (success of this sort would, in any case, probably have harmful effects on his music). On the other hand, with a fair amount of accuracy, he will probably be awarded his rightful place in the scale of cultural values. His is certainly an enviable status by comparison with that of the authentic artist in the world of serious contemporary music, that solitary artist whose very existence is denied by the socially established traditionalists of every school, and who, like Webern, must often wait scores of years for recognition. I am sure that any modern jazz lover would be dismayed at the idea of these official "values" being transposed into the world of jazz, depriving him of the possibility of hearing at, say, the Newport Festival, musicians who have not yet attained a certain "social" recognition: Sonny Rollins, John Coltrane, Elvin Jones, Philly Joe Jones, and perhaps even Thelonious Monk, Miles Davis, Horace Silver, and Art Blakey.

Yet, without being overpessimistic, one may have reason to fear that the most profoundly original jazzmen have a darker future in store for them. We may indeed be heading for a situation comparable to that which prevails in serious music, and for the very same reason, i.e., because artists make new discoveries faster than the public can assimilate them. The gulf becomes apparent after a generation or two, and grows steadily wider as time goes on. Then the question is not whether an artist is sure to become popular, but whether or not he will even be recognized. Certain signs would seem to indicate that this last stage is in the offing. During the past fifteen years or so, we have, in any case, witnessed a phenomenon of "belated recognition" which is all the more disturbing in that it was accompanied, over the same period, by exactly the opposite phenomenon.

True, the now famous series of recordings done by Charlie Parker between 1946 and 1948 did not sell especially well and it was not until they were re-issued that a larger public became aware of the greatness of these works; Miles Davis's famous Capitol records met with an even colder reception, and stayed on the shelf almost as long as Parker's. Yet both these men, apparently doomed to unpopularity, had almost immediate recognition; musicians and critics alike praised them to the skies. When the Bird died, everyone was aware that modern jazz had just lost its greatest soloist. Similarly, Miles Davis's "comeback" at the 1955 Newport Festival was hailed as a major event precisely because the halo of glory attached to his name a few years earlier had managed to survive a period of temporary neglect. This being the case, why did it take fifteen years for the genius of Thelonious Monk to be recognized? This question sums up in a nutshell the whole problem of the future relations between jazz and its audience. Let us therefore examine Monk's case, which seems to be a perfect example of a certain "depopularization" (in both senses of the word) of modern jazz.

"The recent rediscovery of Thelonious Monk," writes Martin Williams, "is surely one of the most curious events in the admittedly short history of modern jazz. The fan and trade press, which once dismissed his recordings with a puzzled or scornful two or three stars, now waxes enthusiastic at the slightest provocation and lists his name in polls where it seldom appeared before. Musicians who once dismissed him as having long since made his small contribution to jazz now listen attentively for ways out of the post-bop and post-cool dilemmas. And the public which had once barely heard of this man with the intriguing name now buys his records and attends his public appearances."[1]

Of course, even when Monk began recording in 1941, his

---

[1] *Evergreen Review,* No. 7, Winter 1959.

style was far too original and far too removed from current practice to be immediately accepted by all. (Moreover, as I have said before, Monk has not yet attained real popularity.) It seems, nevertheless, that beneath certain superficial stylistic features which were then regarded as suspect, the real reason why his recognition was so belated lay in a less obvious side of his music. This delay, I feel, was the penalty he had to pay for the intensity of his renovating efforts, for his mighty break with the past, and the drastic change of scenery which he brought about. Sometimes society imagines that this is the way to punish those who steal the fire from the sky. But Prometheus is not yet nailed to his rock; time has already freed Thelonious Monk.

To my mind, Thelonious Monk's music represents a decisive step toward a *different* jazz, in which the sense of form will assume a major role—not a stereotyped form based upon the outdated notions of symmetry and periodically recurring structures, but an active, living form, "a rigorous and irrational organization," in which discontinuity and asymmetry, those pivotal values of all modern art, will constantly challenge those of symmetry and continuity, thereby creating a new and fascinating dialectic of musical time and space.

These would seem to be the future prospects of an aesthetic conception which is probably to be found, for the present, only in the work of Monk himself; but is it so unreasonable to suppose that Monk represents and expresses, in his own way, the secret aspirations of a whole group of jazzmen? If this is true, if I am not overestimating the powers of attraction of Monk's works, we may expect to see the gulf between "popular" and "advanced" forms of jazz that first appeared at the end of the war, grow even wider. For the moment, the audience for rhythm and blues and the traditional ballad is still, to some extent, interchangeable with that of modern jazz. The barrier separating Sinatra from Garner, or Fats Domino from the "funky" pianists is not insuperable. Many modern jazz soloists began their careers with rhythm and blues bands; and economic reasons have obliged several of them temporarily to return to the popular forms of jazz from which they had escaped. (Others, who are better sight readers, prefer to accompany studio singers whose repertory is tinted with jazz.) Exchanges of this sort would be as unthinkable in a world of jazz based at least partially on the concept of formal abstraction, as they have always been in serious European music, where the only problems that classical and popular composers have in common are those concerning their union. European music has, at times, pointed the way for jazz; we may see the day when advanced and popular jazzmen may co-exist in peace. But the greater the artist's advance over his contemporaries, the less he must expect to be understood by them. The great jazzman of the future may spend his entire life in that isolation which Charlie Parker described in such moving terms.

Is the prospect of a form of jazz in which its origins are but a memory, a cause for hope or alarm? European music also sprang from the masses. It took several centuries for it to reach the level of culture, and it was able to thrive magnificently as such for several centuries more. That art form has achieved universality, even though it first flowered in the gardens of an elite. No one would think of describing the *Ode to Joy* or the opening chorale of the *St. Matthew Passion* as the music of a class. It may be somewhat naive of me, but I feel that jazz, though perhaps suffering a thousand deaths on the way, can follow a similar path, for it carries within itself the key to its own universality. Modern jazz is a specialists' music (Martin Williams quite rightly speaks of "Monk's real virtuosity in terms of specific jazz techniques") but it cannot and must not be a music *for* specialists. Though today it is appreciated only by the happy few, the most advanced jazz has already launched invisible missiles in the direction of its future audience. Will that audience really be larger than it is today? Is it capable of being enlarged ad infinitum? The important thing is that the artist have enough self-confidence to draw the audiences of the future to his music, rather than being drawn—in his desire to communicate at all costs—to the audience of today. Thereby hangs the greatness of jazz, as well as its aesthetic and human significance.

Appendix

Self-Critical Notes
and Other
Particulars

PART ONE

Chapter 1

[1] This chapter was first published as an article in the French magazine *Jazz Hot*, No. 98, April, 1955. The Three Great Men of Jazz to whom I refer are Armstrong, Ellington, and Parker.

Chapter 2

[2] This chapter was first published as an article in the Paris weekly *Arts*, 1958.

Chapter 3

[3] This chapter was first published as an article in *Arts*, 1958.

[4] The allusion to Noone and Mezzrow a few lines earlier refers to a series of polemical articles which appeared in *Jazz Hot* between 1948 and 1952.

[5] I do not know whether or not Duke Ellington was referring to this piece when he wrote, in "A Royal View of Jazz" (*Jazz: A Quarterly of American Music*, No. 2, Spring 1959): "I don't want to be modern. . . futuristic. . . and neither do I want to be hung by the plaintiveness of something we might have done years ago, even with success. I don't want to feel obliged to play something with the same styling that we became identified with at some specific period. I have no ambition to reach some intellectual plateau and look down on people. And, by the same token, I don't want anyone to challenge my right to sound completely mad, to screech like a wild man, to create the mauve melody of a simpering idiot, or to write a song that praises God, if I so desire. I only want to enjoy what any other American artist wants—and that is freedom of expression and of communication with our audience."

If he was referring to my article, then he was probably the victim of a hasty translation which distorted its meaning. This is not the first time that this sort of thing has happened to me.

I therefore hope he will take the opportunity to read this chapter in its present translation.

Still and all, the Duke's definition of freedom hardly seems acceptable in the light of modern philosophy. It was certainly not Nietzsche's approach to the problem, when he put these words in the mouth of Zarathustra: "Tell me not from what thou hast freed thyself, but why hast thou done so." (I am quoting from memory.) Zarathustra was inviting man to enjoy the highest freedom of all, but that freedom is conceivable only in terms of rigor. The existentialist philosophers have defined, far better than I could ever do, the limitations which a free man imposes upon himself. Only the irresponsible artist's freedom is absolute; only rigor can preserve art from anarchy.

Moreover, if Duke Ellington has every right to debase his masterpieces, why do not I have the right to protest against this debasement? After all, anyone should be allowed to criticize a work of art once it has been made public.

PART TWO

Chapter 4

[6] This open letter was first published in *Jazz Hot,* Nos. 82 and 83, Nov. and Dec., 1953. It was addressed to a reader of that magazine whose letter had already been commented upon in an earlier issue (Oct. 1953) by Boris Vian.

[7] We must not forget the date at which this article was written, nor the fact that it was written in France.

[8] Needless to say, this description of critical reflection as I conceived it at the time when I had just completed *Hommes et Problèmes du Jazz* (the original French version of *Jazz: Its Evolution and Essence*) no longer tallies—except for certain points made in the preceding paragraph—with my present viewpoint, as I attempt to define it in the introduction to this book. My reason for publishing this letter *in toto* here is that it constitutes a point of reference enabling us to gauge the

progress made since then. For I need hardly emphasize that the essays published at the end of this book (on Milt Jackson and Monk) which are more strictly aesthetic than phenomenologic, in no way constitute a return to outdated conceptions but rather an effort toward a broader understanding of jazz as such. In certain cases—particularly that of Monk—I have gone so far as to reserve my description of the phenomenon under discussion for another occasion; this approach is justified, I feel, when this phenomenon, over and above its immediate significance, leads to a reappraisal of the very fundamentals of jazz. This approach, which stems from a desire for clarity and concision, is undoubtedly incompatible with the "objectivistic" outlook of *Jazz: Its Evolution and Essence.* In chapter 7, moreover, I make it a point to show what privileges are granted to the artist—but to the artist alone—by virtue of his subjectivity.

This letter is also a description of French jazz circles in the early fifties and constitutes a final farewell to a form of discussion which no longer concerns me.

Chapter 5

[9] M. Henri Bernard, one of the earliest and most estimable jazz enthusiasts in France, is referring to an article in which I wrote that "musical stupidity" was not to be found solely in nineteenth-century operetta, but that it could be very much at home in jazz. As an example I cited the lamentable music played by Willie Smith and Charlie Shavers during a Jazz at the Philharmonic concert, and also referred to the playing of Kid Ory.

The two letters that make up this chapter were first published in *Jazz Hot,* No. 78, 1953.

Chapter 6

[10] This open letter first appeared in 1957 in *Jazz Hot* (No. 125). It refers to a round-table debate which appeared in *Down Beat* on June 27, 1957 under the title "A Jazz Seminar."

An earlier translation of this letter—done by David Noakes—was sent to the editors of *Down Beat,* but they did not publish it.

[11] More precisely: the only *modern* way. But, as Lucien Malson points out, "from Plato to Husserl, by way of Descartes (we need only remember the famous analysis of the piece of sealing wax), all philosophers have termed *essence* that which remains intact despite secondary transformations or accidents." I could therefore refute my contradictors' arguments just as logically on the authority of any classical philosopher.

Chapter 7

[12] This chapter was first published in 1956 as an article in *Jazz Hot,* No. 113.

[13] Fate sometimes displays a sense of humor. A critic may sometimes find that his criticism is applicable to himself. Little did I suspect, while writing this essay, what a stinging lesson it was to be for its author. Only a few days later, my first hearing of Davis's and Monk's *Bag's Groove* was to call into question what I had looked upon as Monk's "failure" and, retroactively, shed new light on his past work. In the face of this glaring truth my "aesthetic convictions" toppled—and my music along with them. Neither Bud Powell nor any other musician has ever "stripped away the husk of Monk's failures" —what a mistake! On the other hand, at one point Monk's work helped *me* to strip the errors away from my own music and set it on a different track. The mistake was in my critical judgment but it was also in my music. This is the "formidable wager" that the musician must take up.

PART THREE

Chapter 8

[14] This chapter was first published in 1955 as an article in *Jazz Hot,* No. 95.

Chapter 9

[15] This chapter was published under the title "Improvisation and Composition" in an anthology edited by Ken Williamson, *This is Jazz*, Newnes, London, 1960.

PART FOUR

Chapter 10

[16] This chapter was first published in 1954 as an article in *Jazz Hot*, No. 87. The recordings referred to all belong to the early periods of Count Basie's band.

Chapter 11

[17] This chapter was first published in 1957 as an article in *Jazz Hot*, No. 126. Hsio Wen Chih has already done a very respectable translation of it for *The Jazz Review*, December, 1958.

Chapter 12

[18] This chapter first appeared in 1954 as an article in *Jazz Hot*, No. 86. The Benny Carter recordings cited as examples were all done between 1933 and 1946.

Chapter 13

[19] This chapter was first published in 1955 as an article in *Jazz Hot*, No. 100; it later appeared in *Down Beat* and still later in Martin T. Williams's book *The Art of Jazz*. This new translation has been gone over thoroughly by the author.

The fact that only five of the LP's released under the title "The Genius of Art Tatum" are discussed in this piece is explained by the date at which it was written.

[20] It should be pointed out that this list is deliberately limited to a choice of melodic themes which would probably have been

acceptable for a man like Tatum. Needless to say, my own conception of the jazz theme is quite different. The best pieces done since the war, from the pure "classicism" of *Bag's Groove* to the most disjunct themes of Monk (*Evidence, Criss-Cross*) —which can hardly be called "jazz tunes" at all—have done much to improve a terrain which used to be rather marshy to say the least.

Chapter 14

[21] This article was first published in 1956 in *Jazz Hot,* Nos. 108 and 109.

[22] Can it be that Jackson's playing is not faithfully rendered on records (or at least on those done before 1956)? Or has his style undergone a further change? Whichever the case may be, I was very much struck, when I first heard him in person, by his capacity for violence in his playing. Today I would probably regard certain moments of exacerbated lyricism as the high points of Jackson's work—in the blues as well as the ballad. He has, moreover, rid his phrasing of the "stiffness" I had observed, while actually his remarkable feeling for accents enables him to produce a very fine swing. Still, the subtitle of this essay—"The Recorded Works of Milt Jackson"—to which I now ought to add "prior to 1956," allows me to publish the text as it stands.

Chapter 15

[23] Part of this chapter first appeared in 1958 as an article in the Paris weekly *Arts;* it later appeared, in its present form (but in a different translation) in *Jazz: A Quarterly of American Music,* No. 2, Spring 1959, under the title "A Renaissance of Ellingtonism."

Chapter 16

[24] This chapter was first published in 1959 as an article in *Jazz Hot,* Nos. 142 and 143.

[25] I am referring to a discussion between Michel Fano, Nat Peck, and myself which appeared in *Jazz Hot,* No. 116, 1956.

PART FIVE

Chapter 17

[26] This chapter is composed of a number of articles published in *Jazz Hot*; the section on Charlie Parker appeared in 1953 (No. 73); Dizzy Gillespie in 1953 (No. 75); Billie Holiday in 1954 (No. 85); Django Reinhardt in 1954 (No. 88); Sarah Vaughan in 1954 (No. 92).

PART SIX

Chapter 18

[27] This chapter was first published (in a different translation and in a slightly different form) in the Newport Jazz Festival Program (1959), later in *Down Beat,* August 20, 1959, and finally, in French, in *Jazz Hot,* No. 152, 1960.

Index